T0157170

THE FORGOTTEN BATTALION

BILL EDMONDS

IUNIVERSE, INC.
NEW YORK   BLOOMINGTON

The Forgotten Battalion

Copyright © 2010 by Bill Edmonds

All rights reserved. No part of this book may be used or reproduced by any means, graphic, electronic, or mechanical, including photocopying, recording, taping or by any information storage retrieval system without the written permission of the publisher except in the case of brief quotations embodied in critical articles and reviews.

The views expressed in this work are solely those of the author and do not necessarily reflect the views of the publisher, and the publisher hereby disclaims any responsibility for them.

iUniverse books may be ordered through booksellers or by contacting:

iUniverse
1663 Liberty Drive
Bloomington, IN 47403
www.iuniverse.com
1-800-Authors (1-800-288-4677)

Because of the dynamic nature of the Internet, any Web addresses or links contained in this book may have changed since publication and may no longer be valid.

ISBN: 978-1-4502-0295-4 (sc)
ISBN: 978-1-4502-0296-1 (dj)
ISBN: 978-1-4502-0297-8 (ebk)

Printed in the United States of America

iUniverse rev. date: 4/12/2010

CHAPTER 1

NEVER VOLUNTEER FOR ANYTHING

"Never volunteer for anything!" I heard this from recruits on their way to be inducted, from men waiting to be processed on the first day in the army and from newly uniformed rookies being lined up in their first formation. Sure enough, the sergeant in charge of those first uneven ranks had as his first order of business the call for volunteers.

"This camp area has to be policed up so it's fit to live in," he declared. "I want ten volunteers to police up the grounds—pick up cigarette butts, chewing gum wrappers, everything you see except grass.'"

There was no response whatsoever to this announcement. It was as if every man among us was deaf. Most of the men, no doubt having seen movies showing soldiers in ranks, were staring straight ahead, but some were so militarily naive they were gawking about at various features of the landscape or even the clouds overhead. It did look a bit like rain.

The sergeant's pointing finger swept over the first five men in the front rank. He shouted "You, you, you, you and you!" He then explained, with an air of exaggerated patience, as if we were probably too stupid to understand what he was trying to teach us, "Now, you see, we have just five men to do the work of ten. These conscientious volunteers will be picking up trash until the sun sets and it gets so dark they can't tell a paper wad from dog turd."

He had no difficulty finding volunteers for the next few assignments and we noticed, nervously, that the jobs were getting more and more undesirable. Soon we were waving our hands eagerly. I joined a group

1

assigned to mop the floors of barracks. I noted with relief that the next group was assigned to clean latrines. There were not enough jobs for everyone, and the unassigned, including the few who had remained resolute in their determination not to volunteer, seemed now to be relaxed, almost smirking with an air of "we told you so!" If so, their jubilation was fleeting. The sergeant bawled out, "All right, you wise guys who didn't volunteer for anything, I'm gonna march you over to the medics and they're gonna thank you for volunteering to donate blood. It's a quarter mile march over there. If you're gonna faint, wait until we get there."

I thought, surely a grown man would not faint at the prospect of having a useful quantity of blood drained from his arm, but an experience the next day confirmed that the sergeant's prediction was entirely reasonable. All the rookies were lined up to receive the required vaccination against smallpox and inoculations against the other common infectious diseases that have wreaked havoc with armies in the past. We had to stand in line for quite a long time and those nearing the head of the line had a clear view of what they were in for. At the moment of truth, each victim found himself between two medical technicians who almost simultaneously stabbed a needle into the sensitive flesh of his upper arms. I later heard it said that the needle in one arm was a prop to keep the recipient from falling over while the more painful shot was being administered to the other arm. Not a joke at the time since soon one of the victims did faint. Two husky soldiers, apparently posted nearby in anticipation of this occurrence, pounced on the fallen soldier and dragged him away out of sight. His collapse seemed to have a contagious effect on the apprehensive witnesses awaiting their turn. Soon we were treated to the disgraceful sight of a fainting soldier who was not even near the end of the line. At least two other close observers claimed they were going to faint and were allowed to leave their places in the line. Lest anyone get the foolish idea that this represented a reprieve from the dreaded shots, the sergeant in charge loudly announced that they would be sent to the back of the line so they would have longer to wait for their shots. Longer to anticipate those painful needles, I thought.

Later we were to become accustomed to being given shots from time to time. I personally was vaccinated for smallpox several times.

The scar from a childhood vaccination was very small and faint. My first vaccination in the army "did not take." That is to say, there was no inflammation, no formation of a scar. A few days after the first vaccination attempt a doctor inspected my upper arm and announced, "No evidence of vaccination."

Foolishly, I spoke up, "But doesn't that mean I'm immune to small pox?" Silly me; to think that I had the right to speak to an officer-physician! After all, I was a mere private. Worse than that, I was a lowly rookie in a brand new, ill fitting uniform. I was the lowest form of army life, therefore assumed to be totally ignorant. The doctor pretended he didn't hear my comment. He directed the nurse standing by to vaccinate me. He didn't even have the courtesy to say "again". He seemed to be implying, I thought, that I had somehow evaded the vaccination a few days earlier and was lying now in an attempt to avoid another.

But the army was going to correct my ignorant state. It was going to teach me how to do simple tasks— for example, how to make up a bed. The training sergeant in charge started his lecture with the statement that we were the most pampered army in the world—we each had a bed with a mattress, sheets and a blanket. He then demonstrated how to arrange these luxury items with forty-five degree folds at the corners, and how to make sure that the top blanket was stretched so tautly a coin dropped on it would bounce like a ball dropped on a hard floor. All very simple of course, but as soon as each man had done his own bed, in what he believed was the prescribed manner, the sergeant tested the tautness of the top blanket by dropping a quarter on it. Needless to say, his quarter usually landed with abut as much bounce as a pebble dropped into mud. After that, without wasting words to say the handiwork was unacceptable, he would seize the blanket and sheets and transform them into a disorderly pile on the bed. I think I got mine right on the third try but some of my fellow rookies spent the rest of the evening struggling to bounce that quarter with the bored sergeant watching, then demolishing their work again and again.

In addition to real concerns, like how to do everything the army way, there were strange rumors circulating that disturbed one and all. Within a few days a real concern had arisen that the army cooks were putting something called "salt peter" into the food of rookies so they would not yearn for female companionship. As a former chemistry student I knew that saltpeter was a component of gunpowder. That this might diminish the libido of a healthy young man sounded like sheer nonsense, but my comrades in arms were so worked up over this rumor, I decided it might be best to keep quiet about my doubts. There was much angry talk about whoever was responsible for depriving men of their manhood. Much later I learned that some version of this rumor probably circulates in every army in the world. Russian troops are said to believe the cooks are doctoring their Borsch. Chinese troops think their tea is being tampered with, and Brazilian soldiers sniff suspiciously at their coffee. The fact, I believe, is that when a man finds himself surrounded by an all male assemblage for a few days his sex drive decreases drastically. The incessant sex talk of soldiers is, perhaps, an instinctive effort to reactivate the impulse. The popularity of "pin up" girls was another effort to recharge the libido.

The conversation also tended to linger on tales of how men could have evaded army service if they had not been too conscientious to do so. One man declared it was a well known fact that if you take a bunch of aspirins and drink several cokes just before your physical exam it will cause your heart to act funny and the doctors will exempt you from service. Another declared that if you want to get out of the army you can get up during the night and pee on the floor in a corner of the barracks. Men who do this are sent for an interview with the psychiatrists and are declared unfit for the service. Another sure way to get yourself discharged, it was said, was to offer sexual favors to an officer or high ranking non-com. Since none of the speakers had actually tried any of these stratagems their listeners were being asked to believe that they were all sincere patriots eager to serve their country.

Other medical maters were up for discussion. A few of our companions had mysteriously disappeared. Rumor (This was called scuttlebutt in the army.) had it that they had been moved to a special medical ward for those having venereal disease. Little concern was expressed about this. The army medics could cure anything, or so it was believed. Those segregated for the cure were probably having as restful time in the hospital, being cared for by attractive nurses, "The lucky dogs!"

Other sex talk was of a more optimistic nature. The young man from Lawrence, Kansas, who had shared a train seat with me on the ride to Ft. Leavenworth, let it be known that he had scored many successes with women. He went on to describe his new interest in life. He had decided members of the Woman's Army Corps, the WACS, were clean and safe. "Their health is protected. They have the same medical examinations we have. "Yes siree, I plan to take a whack at a wac as soon as possible."

Another new soldier who had ridden with me from Lawrence was of Mexican-American background. He was a quiet young man, short but very muscular, who distinguished himself that first night by declaring he had volunteered for the paratroops. Queried as to why he did this he responded simply, "More money." Apparently paratroopers were paid more than regular soldiers. Someone asked him if he didn't know paratroopers are paid more because their training is more dangerous than that of the regular army and their chances of survival are poorer. He answered philosophically, "If it's your time to die, you die."

It should be recognized by now that the Mexican-American is an excellent soldier, fatalistic and fearless. They have served in large numbers in many of our wars. Even the Alamo had among its doomed defenders men of Mexican ancestry, as did General Hood's "Texicans" at Gettysburg. Much later, during the Korean War, the casualty lists, published in California newspapers, listed so many Spanish surnames some people may well have asked, "Has Mexico sent its army to Korea?

Our time at FT. Leavenworth was short. A few days later we were off on a long train ride to Texas. Many hours of rolling along through what most people would consider the most monotonous scenery in North America, the mostly flat farmlands of what was once the tall-grass prairie. A Canadian soldier who was wandering through our coach struck up a conversation with some of my train mates and was heard to declare, while pointing out the window, "this is really an ugly country." Perhaps he was looking for excitement in the form of a fight, but if so no patriotic American rose to defend the honor of his homeland. Actually, I could see his viewpoint if he had come down through the Dakotas, Nebraska and now Kansas—with Oklahoma and Texas still to cross he may have been justified in thinking the whole U S A was flat and monotonous. I didn't know at the time that many Canadians feel it is their duty to express disrespect, whenever the opportunity arises, for the more powerful country that lies beside them and to which they are reluctantly wedded for the foreseeable future. As to the "ugly" land over which we were rolling, I did not know until years later that this was once the "tall grass prairie," the most productive natural region in North America, perhaps in the world, before it was destroyed by the steel plow and transformed into drought haunted fields of corn and wheat.

On this journey through a transformed landscape there was one bright spot for me. The troop train stopped for several hours in Newton, Kansas, home town of the girl with whom I went steady for a while during my senior year at college. We were granted two hours of freedom in this wheat-land metropolis and I dashed into the station for a phone and phonebook. Vicky came to the station to meet me and we spent the time walking about and talking, presumably abut old times at alma mater. For me, the newly minted soldier, there was the additional bonus of pride in parading an attractive young lady for inspection by my envious comrades. We parted with promises to write to one another and I resumed my journey to an unknown destination.

CHAPTER 2

HOT TIMES IN TEXAS

Camp Wallace Texas, simmering in the hest of August, was probably an appropriate place to train soldiers for service in the deserts of North Africa. Salt tablets were provided beside the water fountains and we were advised to take one with every drink if we wanted to avoid heat stroke. Our platoon sergeant seemed somewhat confused about this, sometimes he said "sun stroke" instead of heat stroke, but I suppose it made little difference since both were said to be sure death. They weren't, of course, if properly treated, but soldiers were told simple, easily remembered exaggerations like this in an effort to insure proper behavior. I only recall seeing one victim of this dread condition. One of the old boys, probably in his thirties, collapsed during a hike and I noted his face was fiery red. The medics hauled him away in an ambulance.

Hikes, calisthenics and the obstacle course were expected to turn us into hard-muscled fighting men. Obstacle courses were actually fun for the man who was active enough to negotiate the varied hazards without any of those failures that caused a training sergeant to explode into rage. I recall one training sergeant expressing his amazement about "a bunch of college boys" who went out after a day of hard training to practice running the course again. I have forgotten some of the details of the army obstacle courses of that time but I recall a ladder-like overhead structure where we were expected to swing from cross bar to cross bar like Tarzan of the apes swinging through the jungle trees. There were logs elevated on supports to form hurdles. These were fiendishly spaced so it was almost impossible to recover from one jump before making another. And of course there was "the wall." A soldier in the bloom of youth and health could leap up and grab the top of the barrier with both hands, then pull himself up by sheer arm power while his feet pawed futilely at the smooth wooden surface. He then maneuvered one leg over the wall, rolled his body over the top and dropped down triumphantly on the other side. For many of the older and shorter men, particularly those who had spent years at a desk or on a sales floor, this was simply impossible. But the training sergeants didn't know that word. The man was a soldier now and must perform like a soldier. The sergeant directed a tirade at those who failed. Even though it might have been obvious to an unbiased observer that the man was to small to reach the top of the wall by jumping, the sergeant declared his failure was due to lack of determination, manhood, self respect and every other character flaw the trainer could think of. Furthermore, the delinquent should be in the WACS (Women's Army Corps) instead of this man's army. He needed a mother's care and, "Believe me, the army is not your mother!" We who had finished the course successfully were marched back to the barracks by a platoon leader, the voice of the raging sergeant growing fainter with distance.

We were trucked to an obstacle course of another kind on the beach at Galveston. This featured strands of barbed wire stretched across the course just high enough that a soldier, squirming on his belly like a distressed worm, could wriggle under then. In some places, where the wires were hanging to low for belly crawling, the man had to turn over and hold the wire up with one hand while trying to wriggle forward on his back. His other hand of course was dragging the rifle which functioned throughout as an anchor impeding his progress. But the main feature of this course, the one that demanded his unwavering attention, was the thunderous rattle of one or more machine guns firing bullets just above the wires. The sergeant in charge had explained that if a soldier allowed any part of his body to rise above the level of the wires it would be struck by bullets---painfully if it was his butt, fatally if it was his head. In briefing us for this trial the sergeant declared that he had once seen a soldier leap to his feet yelling, "Snake!" then drop dead, riddled by bullets. "If you see a snake," he said, "Don't jump up, jist lay still and don't do nothing' to aggervate the snake." Later I learned that this story was usually told to soldiers who were about to negotiate the course---the teller often adding interest by claiming he personally had witnessed the calamity. Our group managed to survive this trial; no bullet holes and no snakes.

A principal form of exercise, practiced daily, sometimes for hours, was called close order drill. This was simply marching in an orderly manner, the whole group, usually a platoon of forty-eight men, maintaining precisely its arrangement in ranks, or columns as it marched forward, or to the right, or to the left. At the command "To the rear march!" the whole formation reversed its direction of march, each man performing precisely a sort of dance step by which he whirled about one hundred eighty degrees. If done properly the marcher was still synchronized with the cadence count of the sergeant. This took a great deal of practice, many emotional outbursts from the sergeant in charge, and much embarrassment for those individuals who were alleged to have two left feet. Close order drill I supposed was a very ancient tradition of armies everywhere as it enabled masses of men to travel across country without becoming a disorderly mob and surely in the days of battle with swords and spears the best organized troops, advancing in a highly controlled manner, with every man protected by a companion to his right and his left, had a tremendous advantage over a less well organized enemy. History buffs will recall the Macedonian Phalanx, a mass of men like a huge beast bristling with spears and protected by over-lapping shields, that enabled Alexander the Great to conquer the vast Persian Empire.

In addition to these formal exercises we sometimes found ourselves shoveling dirt, practicing the digging of fox holes and other excavations of unknown purpose. And we attended classes every day, sometimes much of the day. Usually we sat on the grass of a parade ground in a rough circle listening to a non-com who lectured us on some aspect of army life. I thought to myself, those kids of seventeen who dropped out of high school to avoid the boredom of classes must have been surprised to find themselves "back in school" for a much longer school day in the army.

CHAPTER 3

HURRICANE!

The training sergeant, lecturing us on the proper performance of guard duty was quite vehement about one point. "You never yell 'Who goes there?' You heard that in those old movies about world war one. What we say now is 'Who is there? Halt, who is there?"

One of the other phrases in the dialogue he was teaching us seemed really archaic. It was "Dismount and advance to be recognized." The sergeant explained that the person addressed would be dismounting from a car or truck, not a horse."

One of the boys from Arkansas put the whole formula to use on a wet, drizzly morning in October while he was posted to guard duty on the road beside the company mess hall. In the half darkness before sunrise a white truck came rolling along the road. Our hero placed himself at order arms in the middle of the road facing the oncoming truck. When it was at a reasonable distance for hailing he called out, "Halt, who—*is*—there?"

The truck came to a stop and the driver rolled down his window, stuck his head partially out into the cold mist and yelled back, "This is the milk truck! I deliver milk to this mess hall every morning!"

But the boy from Arkansas was going to follow exactly the procedure he had been taught. He called our "Dismount, milkman, and advance to be recognized."

The truck driver leaned farther out the window and gave profane expression to his resentment of being ordered to step out into the drizzle.

"If you can't read the sign on the side of this truck then call the officer of the guard—I want to complain to him anyway about putting a dummy with a gun out here to interfere with my work."

The boy from Arkansas, deciding the time had come for the final line in his scrip, called out, "Pass, Milkman."

I can only remember one occasion when I should have called out, "Halt, who is there?" And the absurdity of directing this ritual challenge at some one I was expected to recognize instantly choked off even the initial "halt." I was on guard duty and (pardon the expression) it was a dark and stormy night. Our camp was on the flat coastal plain inland from Galveston, Texas. Its roads were paved with crushed oyster shells---the white shell road that once was common on the south Texas plain. In a previous hurricane the wind had lifted the shells and blown them against the barracks, "sand blasting" away all the paint on the windward sides of the buildings. Now on this night in late summer of 1943 another gulf hurricane was threatening the area. I was on guard duty, walking my post in the howling wind that seemed to be trying tear my raincoat from my body and rip off my helmet in spite of the chin strap. Raindrops were flying horizontally stinging my face. and my trousers were as wet as if I had been wading in knee-deep flood water. I had been walking back and forth in this deluge for at least an hour when suddenly a well known form loomed out of the maelstrom just in front of me. It was the battalion commander. There was no way I could yell, halt, who is there, at that awesome figure. Instead I came to attention, saluted, held the salute, and said, "I know you, sir." I was immediately embarrassed—it seemed a silly thing to say. But he came right up to me, looking me up and down in the flare of his flashlight, and exclaimed, with noteworthy lack of originality, "Soldier, you're wet as a drowned rat!" Then, to my amazement, he bawled out in a loud voice, "Officer of the guard, post number three."

They must have recognized his voice. The lieutenant who came dashing to the scene was wearing a forage cap, wholly unsuitable for the pouring rain; and struggling to don a raincoat that was whipping wildly in the wind. The sergeant of the guard, right on his heels, was better dressed for the occasion in buttoned raincoat and helmet liner.

The Colonel said, "Send this man back to his barracks to dry out. Pull in all the guards. We're going to patrol with trucks until it gets too difficult to drive."

Back at the barracks there was a flurry of activity. Men had placed packs on the beds, and were transferring essentials from foot lockers to packs as if in preparation to go on bivouac or into combat. An order had come down from headquarters that if the storm worsened we were to don full packs, steel helmets, sling our rifles on our backs and then lie down in the floor between the beds. The platoon sergeant had cheerfully announced that if the barracks started breaking up we would move out into the storm and dig in. Since a previous hurricane had produced a storm wave that had brought sea water over much of the camp, this didn't seem to be a practical solution for our difficulties.

Soon we were decked in full combat equipment, but the order to lie down on the floor never came. After a while the lights were extinguished---or maybe the power failed because of the storm. Since no further orders were given, we simply lay down on our beds, fully clothed, and eventually went to sleep. When we were aroused at the usual hour of five thirty the noise of the storm had ceased. We were ordered to restore our gear to the foot lockers, put the rifles backing their rack at the end of the barracks, and prepare for the usual day of training.

Fortunately for us, the eye of the storm had come ashore somewhere else on the Texas coast. Later I learned that the sergeant's playful announcement, that we would move out into the storm and dig in, was his own variation on the idea that we would make our way to the gun emplacements, huge concrete enclosures in which the big guns of the coast artillery were mounted. The concrete pads on which the guns were standing were high enough to be secure against any storm wave, and the surrounding walls, designed to shield gun crews from the near burst of shells fired by enemy warships, would certainly have withstood the wind of a powerful hurricane. But there would have been no overhead shelter from the pouring rain---a safe but very wet haven for the men.

CHAPTER 4

A HOSPITAL INTERLUDE

My contacts with the Army's medical service sometimes led to memorable experiences. The first of these was with a dentist who, during the routine examination bestowed on all rookies, discovered to his delight that nature had arranged my wisdom teeth in a manner which would cause me trouble in my old age or possibly even sooner. He proceeded to bring forth his hypodermic needles and administered generous doses of anesthetic to both sides of my mouth. As soon as I was satisfactorily numbed, he set to work extracting wisdom teeth. He counted jovially as he worked: "One--- two--- three, that's enough for today." The anesthesia must have worked on my brain as well as on the nerves of my jaws for the next day I had no memory of the actual extraction process. But I had a terribly sore mouth. In addition to the reaction of the outraged gums from which teeth had been summarily torn, I had chewed my tongue and the linings of my cheeks during dinner while still under the influence of the anesthetic.

A few weeks later there was a flu epidemic I awoke one morning with a hot face and aching joints. Unable to eat breakfasts, I reneged on my resolution never to put my fate in the hands of the medics and reported to the company clerk for permission to go on sick call. He was instantly attentive to my condition, snarling "Grab a broom and clean up this office while you're waiting for transportation." I didn't feel like standing up, much less pushing a broom, but this was the army, so I set about pushing.

After a while hospital transportation arrived in the form of a flat-bed trailer towed by a truck. There were several wooden benches mounted on the trailer, the army's open air version of a bus for sick patients. I joined a few other suffering soldiers who were sitting on the benches and reflected that it was unlikely that we would share our germs with one another while that clean, icy wind was cooling our feverish faces. I had repeated sessions of shivering violently with a chill. We waited for what seemed like a long time while the driver of the truck took care of some urgent business elsewhere. We suspected that he had gone to the mess hall for a second cup of coffee to brace him for his hard day's work of collecting sick patients and driving them to the hospital.

Happily, all of us were still alive when the truck and trailer finally drew up to the entrance of the base hospital. There was another wait, this one in a heated room where coughing and sneezing presumably disbursed germs and viruses into the warm air to be shared by all. Finally I was ushered into the office of a young doctor who was wearing the silver bars of a first lieutenant.

He took my temperature and asked if I had aching joints. I eagerly described all my symptoms and at that moment began to shiver with a chill in spite of the warmth of the office. He was seemingly impressed by my quivering frame and chattering teeth and demonstrated his soothing bedside manner by saying, "I think you may have pneumonia. I'll have to keep you here for a few days." He called for a nurse and while we were waiting for her arrival I noted with a twinge of nostalgia that his new medical diploma, hanging on the wall, was from the University of Kansas. I must have been slightly delirious to have attempted small talk with a first lieutenant for I exclaimed, "I was there just three months ago."

He said, "Where? Then followed my gaze to the diploma and became instantly transformed from a haughty, business-only officer into a fellow graduate of dear old alma mater. We chatted in a friendly fashion for a while, reminiscing over the good old days, Kansas co-eds, and memorable pre-game rallies with bonfires lighting up the night and massed voices chanting, "Rock chalk, Jay Hawk, KU! Then he sent me down the hall to a small room with only one bed where attractive nurses with shiny lieutenant's bars seemed unaware that the mysterious celebrity who had been assigned to a private room was actually a rookie.

My contemplation of this new, luxurious life style was soon interrupted by white coated technicians wheeling in a massive x-ray machine. I was required to lie on what seemed to be a large sheet of metal that had just been brought in from the cold out of doors. I must have registered some discomfort because a technician assured me that it would only take a few minutes to photograph my lungs to determine if I was developing pneumonia. Shivering with another chill, I said, 'If I don't already have pneumonia I will have it after this." One of them said, "We'll hurry, Sir." I supposed the rule was, "Say Sir to people in private rooms."

The hospital stay was an agreeable vacation from army life. I recall no symptoms of illness after the first day. The food was good. Soft music came from the P A system. I did a lot of sleeping. One day I was lying there anticipating dinner, as I had nothing else to do, when my first real, live movie actress walked into the room. She came over to the side of my bed, smiling angelically, and asked, "Do you know who I am?"

I thought I did. I blurted, "Mickey Rooney's mother!"

I could see she was not particularly pleased by this answer. She said, rather primly," I am Fay Bainter."

Then she wished me a speedy recovery, and left the room without further comment. After describing this incidnnt later to one of my fellow soldiers I was embarrassed to acknowledge that I had been wrong on at least two counts. Faye Bainter had never played the part of Micky Rooney's mother—that was Spring Byangton—and apparently the only thing these two actresses had in common was a last name starting with a B. But, after all, asking a stranger, "Do you know who I am?" was asking for a possibly wrong answer, wasn't it? And besides all movie actresses of those days, with their heavy makeup under the intensely bright klieg lights, did look somewhat alike.

Besides, my thoughts were probably on one of the nurses who seemed particularly friendly. I had become bold enough to give her my best smile each time she appeared and had been the recipient of a very pretty smile in return. Her's was the only smile I received from that troop of stiff, professional, lieutenant nurses. I complimented her on the skill with which she took my temperature and blood pressure and expressed admiration for her appearance when she came in one day with more make-up than army regulations approved. Once she came in and caught me singing a popular song of the day, "Darling, tell me when, we will meet again, Sunday, Monday or always?"

She said, "I think you're well enough to leave us." I found it a disappointing response to my romantic crooning.

Finally, the order came for me to depart from my happy hideaway and return to the harsh reality of army training.

I extracted my baggy uniform and rough shoes from the closet and dressed with haste, hoping to get out of the area before my favorite nurse saw me out of my disguise as an important patient. I was toying with the idea of putting her on my letter writing list and was sure the relationship, whether real or imaginary, would be blown if she saw me in that grubby private's outfit.

I managed to check out unseen. I walked a half mile or so back to the company area and reported, reluctantly, to the same corporal-clerk who had handed me a broom at our last meeting. He barked at me, "Yer late. The company is already gone for the day's training. Get on over to the mess hall and tell the cook yer on K P for the day."

Soon I was up to my elbows in hot sudsy water , washing an endless procession of dishes and silverware. The usual fierce, critical, cook-sergeant was on duty that day and quickly re-adjusted my mental attitude in accordance with army standards.

CHAPTER 5

GAS!

One of the mysteries of World War Two was why Hitler's *Wehrmacht* never used poison gas. American apprehension about this possibility led to much wasted time and expense in training and equipping our troops. During training hikes we always carried gas masks and any soldier who was caught without this usually useless piece of equipment was in serious trouble if a training sergeant suddenly felt the urge to yell, "Gas!" In most cases this was a false alarm but I remember an occasion when it was for real. A canister of tear gas was released beside our marching column. Our training sergeant apparently had no fore-warning and I can see him now as he turned to face us, his eyes squinted, his features distorted as if by inconsolable grief. He was giving strangled cries of "gas! Gas!"

I suppose most of us managed to get out masks on promptly enough to avoid the kind of suffering he was demonstrating. I kept my eyes tightly closed while I donned and adjusted the mask so I failed to witness any distress on the part of comrades. I suppose that particular practice drill was considered a success."

On another occasion we were deliberately exposed, unprotected, to the unpleasantness of tear gas as part of a training exercise. We were directed to enter, one at a time, into a barracks building where tear gas had been released. A training officer was there, wearing a mask of course. We had been instructed to come to attention in front of him, recite our army serial number, and don our own gas mask only when commanded to do so. After entering the door I had to locate the officer who was standing across the barracks, on the side opposite the door. This meant my eyes had to be opened at least intermittently while I crossed the room. Arriving in front of the officer I stood at attention with tears streaming down my face and recited my eight digit serial number, remembering to punctuate it at the end with a "Sir!"

The officer, in a kindly but unhurried manner, said "Put on your gas mask, soldier". The mask gave no relief at first as the part covering my face was filled with the gassy air of the room but I moved quickly out into the outside air and snatched the mask off.

It was pointed out later that the officer had no way of checking the accuracy of the numbers we gave him. I suppose the critical factor was the confidence with which the victim recited his number. The situation would have been miserable for someone who hesitated, stammered, or had to start over. Later that day I heard one joker say, "I knew my number started with a three, but I couldn't think of what came after that. So I just gave him my girl's telephone number." His story could have been true, a three added to the usual seven digit telephone number would have given eight, the correct number of digits for a serial number. He reported the officer said "That's good, soldier. Put on your mask."

Most of the men snatched off their masks as soon as they were in the outside air, though no order was given to do so. Some men doubled up with violent coughing, a few seemed on the point of vomiting. Even the relatively unaffected looked around through squinted, painful eyes as if disoriented. It was the kind of scene that can throw a training sergeant into a frenzy of rage. When my vision finally cleared my whole field of view seemed to be filled with the red, angry face of a sergeant screaming "Fall in!" Through sheer lung power he finally assembled the resentful men into reasonably straight ranks and we marched away through a refreshing summer breeze that was gratefully inhaled by all.

On a much later occasion, our squad was hiking up a rather steep slope among the scrubby oaks of an Arkansas hillside when the officer in charge suddenly yelled "Gas!" As soon s we had donned our masks he led us down the hill at the jogging pace called double-time. We quickly learned that the heavy breathing associated with physical exertion was incompatible with the restricted air flow of a gas mask. We arrived at the foot of the slope, received the order to remove our masks, and stood there breathing hard . At this point, one of our eager beavers, ever striving to attract the attention of an officer with his soldierly wisdom, said "Sir, since gas is heavier than air, shouldn't we have run up hill instead of down?

The officers glared at him for an instant then shouted "Gas! Follow me" and charged back up the hill we had just descended. We pounded after him, re-donning masks with muffled exclamations of rage. I am not sure who the culprit was---the one who pointed out the officer's mistake--- but if it was Moyer, one of our most memorable eager beavers, it may have contributed to his career advancement. Soon after this he was one of the first in our training group to be promoted to corporal.

CHAPTER 6

PRISONERS OF WAR

As we marched about the base, to and from training exercises, we would see small work groups of husky young men, bronzed by the sun of Africa. They were performing various tasks under the watchful eyes of armed guards. They often stopped what they were doing and stood, staring haughtily as us as we marched by. Our resident German, Klaus Berg, who had attached himself to me as a friend the day he caught me reading a non-fiction book on the ethnic groups of Europe, was the only one among us who expressed hatred for the prisoners. He usually referred to them as "those arrogant bastards." He said when they stared at us they were remembering the propaganda which sneered at Americans as soft, effeminate, and poor soldiers. He said even the quiet thumping of our shoes as we marched, so different from the crashing foot steps of German soldiers shod with hobnailed boots, was considered evidence of our military deficiency. Klaus's bias against his former countrymen was understandable. Son of a German naval officer he had grown up with the expectation of a military career. But in the late nineteen-thirties his parents had become increasingly anxious about a family secret: one of his mother's grandparents was Jewish.

Klaus told me that he and his mother had been able to escape from Germany only because they were aided by the naval officer comrades of his father. He declared the German navy was not as poisoned by Nazi racial theories as was the army.

In spite of my own observations, I seemed to see those prisoners at Camp Wallace through Klaus's eyes. I noted their arrogant stares, the show-off precision with which they marched to and from their camp. They were dressed in American fatigues and shoes. I didn't doubt that they missed those hob nailed boots. Those off duty were always neatly uniformed as if they were ready for inspection. Most surprising to me was their response to the sunset bugle call. Lowering of the big flag over headquarters was accompanied by the somewhat mournful bars of "Retreat"---a recording of a bugle call blaring from multiple speakers scattered over the camp. Like all the bugle calls which marked turning points of the army day, it was said to have been recorded by one of the Dorsey brothers, popular musicians of the era. At the first notes of this call everyone in the camp—from guards on duty to cooks in the kitchen—was required to come to attention facing toward the headquarters flag, however distant, and stand rigidly at attention until the last note trailed away into silence. This ceremony was said to be in remembrance of all American soldiers who have died for their country.

And what did a German prisoner do when the sad notes floated over the camp? He halted where he was, came to attention facing the headquarters stars and stripes, and stood as rigid as a toy soldier until the ceremony was over. Perhaps this was a practice of the German army---our bugle calls inherited from the Prussians by way of Genreral Von Stuben who wrote the first training manual for General Washington's army.

The prisoners were said to lead a comfortable life. They received the same food as our own soldiers. They were paid some token wage for their volunteer labor. They had their own Post Exchange (PX) where they could purchase cigarettes and other small luxuries. There was a rumor that they had petitioned headquarters to provide them with the services of prostitutes. This request was denied, or so the rumor had it, with the explanation that American soldiers were not provided with such a service.

My last sighting of prisoners came at Ft. Leonard Wood Missouri after the war was over. It was mid-winter. There was a spell of bitterly cold weather. When the dinner call sounded we lined up outside the mess hall door and waited to be let into the dining room. We stood in line, wearing our engineer mackinaws with wool caps pulled down over our ears, hands thrust into coat pockets in violation of an army rule, shivering with cold.

Now was the time when the German prisoners who had volunteered to work in the kitchen chose to take a break. They would come out onto the back porch of the mess hall, shirtless, bare shouldered in army undershirts, bare headed in the icy air. They would light up their cigarettes and stand there glowering at us contemptuously, pretending they felt no discomfort from the icy wind whistling past their ears. It seemed clear they were trying to demonstrate that even as prisoners they were still Nazi Supermen.

CHAPTER 7

THEY HAD COMPUTERS?

At last, my college education was going to be recognized! I was suddenly assigned to an electronics school, a very special electronics school, one dealing with a "computer" that would direct the fire of multiple anti-aircraft guns. The first day in class we were informed of the miraculous nature of this device, and how lucky we were to be assigned to its repair and maintenance. I remember that first class meeting because of the abrupt let down which I received in regard to any previous information I had leaned about the wonders of electronics. The instructor asked, "Does anyone know what electricity is?

Now there was a question right up my alley! I was a physics major with special interests in electricity and magnetism. I didn't exactly wave my hand in the air but I did raise it. The instructor glared at me as if I were an intruder from some foreign land and let his expression change gradually from a glare to a sneer. He spoke to the class at large, "Now listen to this!" His sneer had changed by now to a contemptuous half grin to let the members know, I suppose, that a joke was in the offing. He then directed me to sand and speak.

I explained that the atoms of elements that are conductors, such as copper, are surrounded by a number of loosely held electrons which can be forced to stream from one point on the conductor to another by an electromotive force, produced by a generator which uses swiftly moving magnets to impart motion to the stream of electrons, or by chemical cells, called a battery, in which a chemical reaction moves electrons from one plate to the other creating a surplus of electrons on the negative plate and a deficiency of electrons on the positive plate—.

At this point the instructor roared, "Sit down soldier!"

I dropped into my seat amidst amused laughter from my comrades. And the instructor, whose expression had now reverted to the original stony glare, roared, "Nobody knows what electricity is!"

So much, for the intellectual give and take of an army class room. The brain of a buck private must be a ta*bula rassa,* empty of prior knowledge, ready to receive and retain the wisdom imparted by anyone wearing stripes on his sleeve or metal on his collar.

CHAPTER 8

COLD DAYS IN MARYLAND

It was the winter of 1943-44 and we men from Camp Wallace, Texas, had been "shipped" to Fort Meade, Maryland. We had been sent north by railroad, leaving the mild, damp winter of the Texas Gulf coast and landing here in a place that seemed about as salubrious as Labrador.

It was November, and a bleaker environment would be hard to imagine. The drab barracks buildings were surrounded by acres of dead grass and mud. I was among strangers again. The men from Texas were scattered about in various barracks and everyone seemed absorbed in his own discontent. There was little effort to make new friends. Ours was a special bitterness produced by being treated again as rookies. So far as the training cadre of this camp was concerned we were all new to the army. If our records had accompanied us to Ft. Mede no one had bothered to read them. We had left Texas with basic training finished and with attendance in specialty schools completed. But now we were here, lost souls in a dismal purgatory, apparently starting our army careers all over again.

There were a few bright spots.—Richard Willis, also from Kansas, a friend from the time of our induction at Ft Leavenworth, sought me out though he had been assigned to a barracks far away. We made plans to go to town together when and if we were released from our unjust confinement. So long as we were considered rookies we were thought unfit to represent the U S Army in public. We might bring disgrace to the service by leaving a jacket flap unbuttoned, wearing a cap at the wrong angle or even commit some forbidden act like sharing, or just carrying, a girlfriend's umbrella

Klaus Berg , my German emigrant friend from the Texas camp, was in a nearby barracks. When we were finally released Klaus invited me to Baltimore for dinner with family friends. We rode a train into Baltimore and took a street bus to near their address. I though the Baltimore residential streets with their rows of town houses; apparently sharing walls with no yards between, were as strange as if I were in a foreign country. Klaus guided me to a pleasant home in a good suburb where a middle-aged man and woman, both small and dark haired, greeted me with formality and reserve. Soon we were seated for a sumptuous meal of food that was completely foreign to me. The man and woman both spoke with German accents. I supposed they were speaking English as a courtesy to me. The conversation, about other friends known to Klaus, was international in flavor. It went something like this---the names are fictitious: "What became of the Goldbergs? Oh, they are living in Algeria now. And did you know the Steinmans got to London---they are doing very well there. . And the benjamins? Ah, they were in Vienna---but we have heard nothing of them since thirty seven.

The woman asked Klaus, "Is it true your mother was an air-raid wardeness in Berlin? It is hard to believe a Jewess could have been given that position."

I thought Klaus's response sounded a bit grumpy. He said, "She is, after all, the wife of a retired Admiral."

The lady asked me where my home was. Smiling, she said to Klaus, your friend looks like a Prussian. I assured her I had no Prussian affinities that I knew of. Her comment amused me because I had early on decided that Klaus was a Prussian prototype. He was intent on becoming a military man, and had the blue eyes, blond hair and fair skin of the ideal (Hitler's ideal) Aryan type.

After dinner Klaus, the big city boy from Berlin, insisted on taking me, the country bumpkin from a small town in Kansas, to my first burlesque show. I thought the costumes were ridiculous, the girls on stage vulgar and unattractive, and was amazed that the loudest applause came from women in the audience. But then I recalled that a sociology professor had mentioned this phenomenon during a class lecture. He implied he found it mysterious that the women were so intrigued. It seemed to me they were simply enjoying vicariously, and safely, the thrill of exposing themselves to the gaze of lecherous men.

We caught a late bus back to camp. Weekends were fleeting. The army week was long and arduous. "Forced march tomorrow," bellowed the training sergeant. "You shitheads are lucky this time. No packs. Just rifles and helmets." I had been repeatedly shocked at the language of non-coms in this eastern camp. I cannot recall that the training sergeants in Texas called the men under them insulting names. I later learned that men from the first service command (New York City and New Jersey) used expressions like "You bastard" or even "You son of a bitch," during casual conservations with friends. I observed that southern boys, which includes Texans of course, only apply such terms to one another when they are angry enough to fight. Both expressions are taken as insults to the mother of the recipient. The first means "Your mother doesn't know who your father was," and the second means literally, "Your mother is a female dog." Both of these are battle cries anywhere south of the Mason and Dixon line and likely to lead to black eyes and lost teeth.

Back to the Sergeant who was bad-mouthing us: He was simply announcing what the army called a "forced march." This, we learned involved fast walking alternating with jogging. I can't remember the length of that march, but I seem to recall that twelve miles was a tyical distance for sch a march. The M1 rifle, sling on my back, thumped me painfully as I ran. The steel helmet became a heavy burden for a runner's neck as the miles went by. The training sergeant seemed to know only one command: "Pick up the pace!"

On a later hike we marched at night in pouring rain along a country road bordered with the white wooden fences of horse pastures. A civilian car came rolling along the road beside us. A soldier yelled at the driver, "You lucky stiff! You don't know how lucky you are!"

I would plod along under the forty pound pack, nine pound rifle and three pound steel helmet in a sort of trance, my well-trained feet and legs carrying me on and on, while my mind wandered in a half-dreaming state.

27

Then there was a twelve mile forced march in a cold winter rain. No pack this time, the rifle slung muzzle down, the helmet and raincoat supposedly protecting us from becoming soaked. When ordered to double time we ran faster than usual, trying to get the ordeal over with. Absurdly we were ordered to take a break. We stood, in the middle of the road the water streaming off our helmets and raincoats.   S o m e men actually managed to light cigarettes in the downpour.

I can't remember at what point I made the sobering discovery that what we were engaged in here was advanced infantry training. Months ago there had been that interview about my physics major, the encouragement to apply for signal corps officer candidate school, then the electronics school in the anti-aircraft battalion in Texas. But we were the last class in that school and the instructor declared we might not be needed for the specialty we had been trained for because "The German air force is out of gas." Now apparently I had been reduced to the most unspecialized and most numerous kind of soldier—the infantry rifleman.

Of course there were other activities besides hikes. Village combat training produced a vivid memory. The course was an area covered with vacant, wooden buildings, simulating a town. One squad at a time, we would crawl up to a building, the sergeant leader would hurl a concussion grenade through the window and the chosen man or men would rush to the window and leap through into the smoky interior. Rifles were at the ready and loaded but we were under strict orders not to fire them. That would be dangerous to men who were ahead of us on the course.

Now it was my turn to charge the window. The sergeant delivered his usual harangue about not firing, ordering us to check to see if the safety was on. He threw the grenade, it exploded with a loud thump inside the room and I was up and dashing for the window. I leaped through, fell to my knees and was scrambling up when a second man came charging through behind me. I had noticed him before, a hillbilly type with a slightly brutal face. When dressed for Saturday inspection he had displayed an expert rifleman's badge pinned to his shirt. It was easy to imagine him as a prototype of those men who have made the U S infantry an awesome force, starting with the skilled marksmen of Morgan's Virginia Riflemen who coolly executed British officers, shooting them off of their horses, at the battle of Saratoga.   N o w this latter day backwoodsman came through the window back of me firing his M1 as rapidly as he could pull the trigger---blam, blam, blam. I was so shocked at his disregard for the sergeant's order that my own danger from this trigger-happy rustic seemed of secondary importance. There was a pause of only a second or two before the sergeant, his face distorted with rage, came soaring through the window screaming, " Who fired that gun?"

Believe it or not, the thought that then ran through my mind was: he told us never call a rifle a gun. Finally my thoughts turned to how lucky I was to have a cold rifle barrel. For the sergeant had grabbed the barrel of the shooters rifle then jerked his hand away from the hot metal. He checked my rifle and found it innocently cold. He then turned his fury on the shooter. He had no further interest in me since I was standing upright and not bleeding. I quietly exited through the window and faded back into the little cluster of fellow soldiers now waiting for the exercise to continue. Most of them seemed unconcerned about both the unauthorized gunfire and the roars of rage coming from the aggrieved sergeant. Perhaps all of us were maturing as soldiers. In the day to day routine of a training camps there is no praise for men who do things right. I could only hope that the sergeant would remember me to the extent of not sending me through that hazardous window again. He did. No doubt the eager shooter was punished for disobeying an order. But I doubt that it interfered with his career as an infantry rifleman. The army needed men like him.

The routine of our lives was not all work. There was play also. One rainy day we reported to the volley ball court for a game in ankle deep mud. I exaggerate only slightly the depth of the mud. Since it was hard to stand up in the slippery stuff, some of us measured its depth by falling down and burying our hands in the muck. But apparently we had become inured to the cold. Every day we sat on bleachers in the icy wind for hour-long lectures and so far as I know no one developed pneumonia.

Grenade practice left me with another vivid memory. We had practiced this in Texas, first learning to throw dummy grenades. We were taught not to throw them like baseballs but to lob them high so they would drop down on the target from overhead.   Eventually each trainee had to pull the pin on a live grenade, then throw it over a barrier of piled up earth, ducking down behind the barrier before the explosion. It is said that training grenades have less explosive power than those issued for combat. We were told we had only four seconds to get rid of the grenade after the pin was pulled and the handle was permitted to fall off.

Now at Ft. Mede we went directly to a more realistic performance. We were to throw grenades from fox holes. These holes were at least five feet deep and rather a tight fit for the two men who were assigned to each one. Before we descended into the holes we were harangued by the training sergeant in a manner that didn't build confidence. He said, "If you drop the grenade after you pull the pin, don't try to climb out of the hole. It's been tried and nobody has ever made it. If you drop the grenade, you have to pick it up and throw it." I had a vision of two men in tight quarters scrambling and bumping heads in a frantic effort to pick up the armed grenade and throw it before it exploded.

Well, I had thrown a grenade before. I certainly didn't plan to drop it. But now a problem emerged over which I had no control. My companion in the fox hole, a young soldier I had not seen before, was apparently terrified. His hand holding the grenade was trembling and his face was white. My vision of two men scrambling fruitlessly to grab and throw a dropped grenade came into sharper focus. I am sure I must have been holding my breath as he struggled to pull the pin, dropped the pin (that falling pin was in itself a shocking occurrence—ike a preview of what he might drop next!)), then did a hasty but feeble throw which accomplished little more than if he had simply shoved the grenade out over the edge of the hole.. The sharp, ringing "Pow" of the explosion—someone said it was like a bell exploding—was very close and deafening but I heard the ping of a fragment on someone's helmet, either his or mine. I supposed a fragment blown high into the sky had dropped back upon us.

I asked my companion to crouch down out of my way—a suggestion he responded to eagerly. I pulled the pin, and threw my grenade in the prescribed manner. It exploded and the sergeant came rushing up to direct his rage at my inept companion. I think I was wondering at that point if German or Japanese soldiers in my future would be more dangerous than some of my present companions.

CHAPTER 9

THE RACE AND THE PRIZE.

Then came the forced march that almost changed my life. The weather was good and I was feeling very fit from the hard training. Our leader this time was a powerful looking professional athlete type, not a sergeant but an actual officer, a captain. He was, I thought, probably one of those star football players who were given commissions and assigned to the physical training of soldiers. But he was a gentleman, actually shouting encouragement to those poor devils who were struggling to keep up, the old men, those in their thirties.

I don't remember how far we marched that day but about a quarter mile from the finish we who were long of limb and young in age had been sorted into the front of the column. The captain came jogging up to join us and called out, challenging us to beat him to the finish line. I had run the quarter and half mile in high school. Nothing spectacular, although my mile relay team had gone to the state track meet—where we ran last against B-class (small) high schools! So I sprang forward and tried to reactivate my quarter miler's pace. There were footsteps pounding behind me—five or six of my fellow hikers, I later learned. I like to think I set the pace for them—on a race of that length, too much speed at the beginning leads to exhaustion before the end. No doubt our time for the quarter mile was poor. The rifle and steel helmet insured that. But when we reached the company office and collapsed on the steps the captain was well behind us. He was built to be a tackle or a guard, I thought, not a fast end. We made a gesture toward getting up when he arrived but he said, "At ease men," and we sank back to the boards. I think he would have liked to sprawl beside us. He stood there panting hard for a minute or so, then gasped, "You men go into the company office." I wondered if we had misunderstood and were going to be disciplined. I think we were too tired to care. We stood there in the office breathing hard, probably looking glum. The captain came in. He had assumed the air of a coach, pleased with the performance of his team. He actually grinned at us. "Good race, fellows, he said." He then informed the startled company clerk that we were to receive passes to go into town that night."

After he left the office the clerk, a small man in his thirties with steel-rimmed army issue glasses, said "That's our new company commander. Boy, I wish I were built like him."

A pass on a weekday night was unheard of except for members of the training cadre. It seemed like a hollow reward to me. I was surely too tired to ride the bus to Laurel, Maryland, stand in the cold for some unknown length of time until the train came, then ride into Washington D. C. Then what? Start planning how to get back to camp in time for morning roll call. But I showered and dressed and sprawled on my bed wishing I weren't so tired.

The platoon sergeant came in and announced that a bus had been arranged for those men who had been awarded a pass for this evening. "The bus will take you to a USO dance, then pick you up at midnight and bring you back. Can you beat that? A dance, you know, with girls. Real, live girls, remember?"

Many of my fellow soldiers were prone to sneer at U S O dances. "Prudish, middle class girls," Klaus would have said.

And the U S O girls had given a pledge not to date the service men they met—surely one of the most widely broken pledges in history. But they were just my speed. The Houston, Stage Door Canteen had been, so far, my closest approach to heaven. Praise the Lord for bestowing on Texas its one redeeming glory: Legions of tall, shapely, blonde girls.

I got up off the bed and went to the mirror in the latrine to check my uniform and the angle of my cap. I had a gaunt and hollow cheeked look, like a Civil War Soldier in one of those old photographs by Mathew Brady—or a distance runner in peak condition. I went out to find the bus.

We were delivered to a building with a large dance floor. I never thought to ask where it was. Probably in Arlington. She was from Arlington. I stood looking over the crowd---a big crowd. The floor was really too crowded for dancing. I was too tired to dance anyway. Soldiers, sailors, lots of girls.- Middle class girls, well dressed, every hair in place, lipstick artfully applied. The music stopped; some dancers left the floor and some simply stood. There were so many girls some of them had been dancing with each other. I saw a tall blonde, reminiscent of a warm night in Houston. Maybe just one dance I thought. I started pushing my way toward her, working my way through the crowd. There was a girl with her, a shapely girl with dark brown hair. She turned her face toward me, saw me, thought I was coming to her. It was a face as familiar as that of my own sister—I could never understand why this was so. Big brown eyes in an alert, intelligent face—a face just short of beautiful. Lighted now with a welcoming smile, it was beautiful. The music had started. I reached for her, she held out her arms, the blonde was forgotten.

What did we talk about? Bits of memory remain. We chuckled at the silly song—Mares eat oats and does eat oats, etc. I told her I was going to be a science teacher. She said she had made an A in high school chemistry. She was working for the Navy, in Washington, in one of those temporary buildings on the mall. She said her name was Frances, "But friends call me Frankie." She said I looked tired. I said I am. We sat together near the entrance. I asked for her address and phone number. She gave it willingly—so much for the pledge. We sat there, side by side, for a while without talking. I think I was too tired to talk and she understood. I caught her looking at me with an expression on her face that startled me. I struggle for the words to describe it. Was it like the expression of a mother looking at an adored child? The bus came. We said goodbye—politely.

The next weekend I got to town again on Saturday morning. I called her from union station. She said "Oh, golly, I promised to go—" somewhere else. She sounded upset.

I left the station and took a bus downtown. The daylight hours brought nothing worth remembering but that evening I went to a U S O, met another girl---about whom I remember nothing except that she was small and dark-haired. I walked her home. She gave me her phone number. But I never saw her again. I didn't see her again because during the week a letter came from Frankie, saying: I had you paged in Union Station right after you called, but I guess you didn't hear it. "I cancelled what I had planned for Saturday. Anyway, I hope you had a good time. I hope you are o. k."

I didn't wait for the weekend--I found a pay phone at the P X as soon as the days training was over and called her. We talked for a long time. Somewhere in that conversation she said, "When I couldn't reach you last Saturday I cried all day."

The import of that statement hit me hard. It seemed to me that without actually saying the words, she had found a way to say "I think I Love You." From that moment I believed she was the girl I would come back to when the war was over.

CHAPTER 10

ANOTHER KIND OF OFFICER

I expected to be sent directly from the advanced infantry training at Ft Mede to the front in Europe or to the South Pacific, but again some mysterious entity, perhaps a yawning clerk sleepily sorting cards at a desk in Washington, or maybe an actual officer reading some compendium of background information that listed me as a physics major, transferred my card to a different file, that of a new combat engineer battalion to be mobilized and trained in a place far from any port of embarkation.

So, suddenly I found myself on a train headed for I knew not what or where. I only knew the train was headed west and as the hours went by the chance that we were going to an eastern port faded away. Were we headed for San Francisco and the Pacific theatre of war? Night fell, the train rolled on and on. When I awoke next morning, after a night of restless sleep in the seat of a railway coach, the train had stopped at a small station. I looked out into the dim light of pre-dawn to see an officer pacing up and down, staring at the train as if concerned about some cargo it was carrying. He may well have been concerned. It was his responsibility to meet a contingent of raw troops and take them in charge. His helmet bore the vertical stripe of white paint that simulated the bar of a first lieutenant and the name "Jacks." I thought it a curious name. Jack is a common name for a man but I knew "Jacks" only as a game played mostly by girls. They bounce a ball and pick up "jacks," small metal objects, while the ball is in the air. It was claimed to improve their dexterity making them more efficient at working with their hands.

It seems doubtful that it improved anything other than their skill at playing jacks.

In any case, the officer's name was Jacks and he was there to greet the makings, the raw material, of the headquarters company of a new engineer combat battalion. I suspect he was surprised at the alacrity with which we "fell in"— assembled into ranks—to be marched to the trucks that had come to pick us up. It was later rumored that he was expecting untrained men, fresh from a reception center—clumsy rookies with both feet still in civilian life. Instead, many of the men who filed off the train were from the Army Special Training Program (ASTP) and had been on college campuses learning special skills for a number of months—as well as the special army skills, like marching. Later I heard that before boarding the train, the ASTP men were enjoined by the officer in charge to conduct themselves at all times as befitted future officers of the United States Army. But at the end of the ride they found they were beginning basic training again, buck privates all, and expected to compete for weeks for the coveted stripe of a private first class or a corporal. The god-like status of an officer seemed as hopelessly unattainable as on our first day in the army months earlier.

Every day the lesson is driven home that officers are infallible and must be treated with the kind of respect a lowly serf displayed for his lord in feudal days—a humbleness completely foreign to the American psyche. And certainly most training officers seemed quite willing to play the role of an aloof, superior being, too exalted even to speak directly to an enlisted man. They stand silent and apart while their selected spokesmen, the training sergeants, bull voiced, poorly educated and prone to rage, remolds the callow trainees into a soldier.

So we set about re-learning all the skills that are taught in the first six weeks of army life: how to march in formation, how to do the "manual of arms," how to identify enemy planes, how to avoid venereal disease, how to pitch a two-man tent, how to stick together as a squad on a night patrol, how to read a compass, how to care for our feet before and after a long hike, all at a level that seemed like kindergarten following the training we had already had. Needless to say we did remarkably well at learning all of these skills.

We did quite a bit of hiking. Lieutenant Jacks emerged as our hero on the day of the twenty mile hike. We enlisted men were heavily laden as if for battle. Each man carried a full pack, emergency rations, a canteen full of water, a shovel for digging foxholes, and of course a rifle and steel helmet. We noticed resentfully that most of the young officers who accompanied us carried only small musette bags on their backs and holstered pistols on their belts. It was widely believed that officer's packs were loaded with empty cardboard boxes. It was pointed out that round oatmeal boxes, end to end and wrapped in a piece of blanket could be used to simulate a bed roll. It seemed significant that the officers did not bother to remove their packs during the break periods. They stood and talked to one another, puffing their cigarettes, showing no symptoms of fatigue, while we enlisted men sprawled on the grass, red faced and sweating, our heavy gear on the ground beside us. But Lieutenant Jacks was laden just as we were. We watched him remove the pack at the beginning of a rest period and heave it back into position with obvious effort when the order came to march on.

As we slogged away the weary miles the company stretched out into a long single file. The one hundred forty men of Headquarters Company had many stragglers with painful feet. Once an ambulance came rolling up the road and stopped to pick up a man who had collapsed. Probably another case of heat stroke. It was a hot afternoon.   Throughout the march, Jacks repeatedly left his position in the lead to walk back along the line of march, peering at each individual soldier as if checking his condition. He apparently continued his march to the rear until he had checked on the last straggler, after which he jogged forward again to the head of the line. I wondered how many miles he was traveling as we trudged our assigned twenty.

Toward the end of the hike we passed a large detachment of infantry resting beside the road. Jacks began to sing; a tuneless and ridiculous song that I had never heard before. With that same serous look on his face he shouted out the words.

"Oh, what would the army do without the engineers? Can anyone tell me what they would do? The infantry may think that we are just a bunch of queers. But where would the infantry be without the engineers?"

He yelled, "Everybody sing," then repeated the words as those near him joined in. The infantry men began to jeer at us—which inspired us to sing louder. Soon our whole procession of very tired men was shouting the silly song.

At the end of the hike the company was re-formed on the parade ground, those men who finished first waiting, sitting or sprawled on the grass, until the last straggler arrived. That straggler was accompanied by Lieutenant Jacks. The lieutenant came striding onto the scene, showing no evidence of being tired. He was greeted with hand clapping and cheers, which he accepted without change of expression. For the enlisted men of a training camp to cheer and applaud for one of their officers, especially at the end of a day of harrowing effort, is probably a rare occurrence in military life.

After a few weeks I was assigned as the understudy to a staff sergeant bearing the impressive title of mechanic foreman. He had been accepted to officer candidate school and it was implied that when he left, I would assume his job. My first tasks were mostly of a clerical kind, checking training schedules for errors and conflicts, running errands for officers, nailing up signs to guide units on practice missions, important stuff I'm sure but nothing calling for heavy thinking on my part. I simply did what I was told to do each day and tried to look alert and interested in what I was doing. But the whole thing fell apart when a staff sergeant, a replacement, was assigned to the company. He claimed that he was the sole survivor of an engineer company that had been wiped out at Kasserine Pass in Tunesia. As a staff sergeant who had held the position of mechanic foreman in his old unit he was a shoe-in for the job I had been training for. I was transferred to the motor pool as an electrician and promoted to corporal—perhaps the promotion was intended as solace for the loss of the promotion to sergeant technician I had been anticipating. An unlikely presumption—the army never provided solace for anyone.

At the opposite pole from Lieutenant Jacks there was one Lieutenant B., whose attitude and demeanor seemed impossible to explain. Surely, absent minded men do not make it through West Point or any of those officer candidate schools that were cranking out officers under the pressure of wartime need. His talent for committing bloopers were evident long before that fatal day when he distinguished himself before the whole battalion.

That was the day of the very special inspection. We had a new battalion commander and he was to be introduced to his command in a program of great formality. For this affaire the whole battalion was assembled on the parade ground. All were freshly bathed, shaved and clean-uniformed. We were arrayed in rows of platoons along each side of the field.

Each platoon consisting of four rows of men, each row a squad of twelve. Four platoons composed a company, four companies a battalion—over eight hundred men when officers and noncms are included—all standing in perfect alignment, ready to snap to attention. Our new leader called out the command, stretching each syllable into a long singing note "Bat-tal-yunnnn, at- ten- shun! Four company commanders echoed him, yelling "Attention!" Sixteen platoon sergeants screamed "tench-hut!"

Eight hundred men snapped into rigidity, standing straight as ram rods---even their eyeballs aligned looking straight ahead, ---rifle held in front of body, barrels pointing straight up. This was followed almost immediately by the command 'Parade Rest". Almost eight hundred rifle butts struck the ground, each man assumed an equally rigid pose, griping the barrel of his rifle with his right hand just below the muzzle, the weapon now slanting forward at just the right angle. Sergeants and corporals of the training cadre were at the ends of the squads. Each company commander was out in front, facing his company, scanning them with either a real or a contrived scowl. Woe be unto the malingerer who failed to present a picture of military perfection.

For some unknown reason Lieutenant B. had taken the place of our usual company commander. This was not surprising as there is a certain fluidity about commands in a training battalion. Perhaps the junior officers were learning various roles. But Lieutenant B. didn't seem to be taking his assignment seriously. He had a half grin on his face and was running his eyes up and down our ranks with the air of a Boy Scout leader about to congratulate his troop on the number of merit badges they have earned. His aspect was so agreeable I felt like smiling. But of course I didn't. Soldiers standing in ranks for inspection are well advised to maintain a warlike scowl.

Now the battalion commander is coming down our side of the field on a course that will bring him in front of our company. He is accompanied by a coterie of senior officers all wearing the expressions of stern dignity appropriate for their rank and for their importance to the vast project that has brought us all to this place: winning world war two. As this awesome personage approaches the front of the first company, the one to our left, the company commander does a snappy about face so that his back is to his men. Then he stands at attention, salutes and holds the salute as the more exalted ones pass in front of him. Now it is B's turn to perform the same maneuver but instead he continues to stand there with a dreamy look on his face, his eyes seemingly focused on some object in the air over our heads. Our master sergeant is beginning to make hissing sounds. In a horse whisper he says, "Sir, about face!" Since nothing happens he continues to whisper, "Dammit lieutenant--sir, about face---for Chris' sake, turn around!" Lieutenant B. seems not to hear this helpful suggestion. Now the inspectors are moving in front of the left side of our company and one of the officers accompanying the Colonel calls out sharply, "Lieutenant B.!" Incredibly, B. turns his head, looks back over his right shoulder at the approaching officers and says "What?"

Nervous giggling breaks out in our ranks. The sergeant begins to hiss again , " Quiet—yer at attention! Quiet. Shhhh—Shut up!" Gradually, a sober hush falls over our ranks. Everyone is probably thinking, as I am, that there will surely be punishment meted out to our company. Will we be denied week-end passes? Will we be assigned to extra duty? It is not our fault that B. has apparently lost his marbles—but we shouldn't have giggled. There is probably a rule in the soldiers' training manual that expressly forbids giggling while standing in ranks.

As a matter of fact we heard nothing more about the incident. But we never saw Lieutenant B. again. His fate as well as the reason for his erratic behavior remained a mystery. There was a running joke about soldiers who obtained a discharge by virtue of "section eight." A soldier who was discharged from the army because of mental problems was referred to as a "section eight." I think it more likely that Lieutenant B. had a drinking habit. I say this because another officer in Headquarters Company who showed actual symptoms of drunkenness while in command of troops was removed from his position and given a less desirable assignment. But he had only demonstrated drunken behavior in front of a few soldiers—not the battalion commander and a whole battalion of troops! Lieutenant B. may have been "broken down" to a common soldier, as well as removed to a different unit.

CHAPTER 11

TROUBLES IN THE RANKS

I remember another occasion when I stood at parade rest for an inspecting general and almost met disaster in a wholly unexpected manner. I was sanding in the front rank of my platoon and we had been at "parade rest" for somewhere between five and ten minutes. The inspecting general was one who had gotten wide publicity over an incident early in the war. He had punished a large number of soldiers because a few of them had whistled their appreciation for the appearance of some young women in shorts on a golf course where the general was playing at the time. The men were in a passing convoy of forty trucks. The offended general demanded that they finish their journey on foot. This involved a march of fifteen miles in the torrid heat of a Tennessee summer. When the news of this punishment reached the public there was a strong reaction against the general which threatened, but probably did not damage, his career.

Now he was here, right in front of oour company, beaming at us and remarking quite audibly to a another officer, "My, this group turned out well!" He was elderly, overweight, with a plump face and was smiling in a most unmilitary manner. I was reminded of an elderly lady admiring her neighbor's petunias.

A few minutes later I became aware that my right hand, rigidly holding the leaning rifle, was growing numb. I was horrified—my hand was going to sleep! A few more minutes of immobility orthe command to "right shoulder arms," and I would surely drop my rifle. Perhaps one has to be a soldier to realize what a horrible blooper it would be to drop your rifle while in formation. I suspect it would be looked upon by authority as equivalent to throwing away your weapon while in combat. Even worse, It might be interpreted as a bid for a section eight discharge from the army.

Punishment for such an infraction was hard to imagine but permanent K. P. duty comes to mind. Frantically I tightened my grip on the rifle barrel—then slightly relax it ---then tighten it again. A dangerous procedure in itself since the sergeant might see that I was moving my fingers and invoke the rule against any motion whatsoever while standing at parade rest. Fortunately I managed to survive a few more minutes during which the inspectors moved away and the sergeant gave the command "At ease," which freed me to reach over with my left hand and steady the rifle. Never was that particular command more welcome.

I have wondered much about this strange phenomenon of having an essential body part go to sleep just when it is performing a critical duty. I think it may be related to that strange phenomenon famously demonstrated by British soldiers being inspected by the Queen. Suddenly a man falls to the ground in a dead faint. This provides an opportunity for the queen to demonstrate that her poise is completely unflappable as she pretends not to see the prostrate soldier. It may also provide an amusing photograph for the next day's news. It must be terribly embarrassing for the fainter when he recovers and has to face amused companions and angry non-coms.

CHAPTER 12

LITTLE ROCK, ARKANSAS

Our engineer camp was near the city of Little Rock, the capital of Arkansas and a very southern city. Perusing the memorial statues around the capitol building I found the impression strong that the Confederacy had won the civil war. The U S O was crowded on Saturday nights with happy couples, soldiers and local girls dancing to popular songs of the era. Our Engineer Headquarters Company soon began to consider a bar called The Brass Rail its official meeting place in the city. In fact much later in England and Europe, whenever we were in one location long enough to set up a canteen or recreation room a sign was hung proclaiming it "The Brass Rail."

In Little Rock I seldom had to use public transportation. Almost always when I was waiting by a bus stop a civilian car would come sliding up to the curb and a friendly voice would call out, "Can I give you a ride, soldier?" Yes, Little Rock in that year of total war was a haven of warmth and hospitality—Southern Hospitality—for the lonely soldier far from home and family. The U S O was awash with attractive girls, there to give soldiers and sailors a sample of the happiness they could anticipate when the war was over. Welcoming smiles greeted us everywhere. We found free food, free transportation, free entertainment and cordial respect from all civilians. Some of the men in my outfit, hailing from teeming eastern cities where smiles are seldom seen on crowded streets, paid Little Rock the highest compliment of all, vowing they would come back there to live after the war was over.

But one hot afternoon in August I saw the other face of the city. I boarded a street bus that was crowded, the aisle packed with standing people. I pushed on board and found I had to stand beside the driver, becoming for the moment the foremost unit in the mass of compressed humanity. Then I realized one more soldier had squeezed in back of me just before the door closed. He was a nice looking young man with a serious face, clad in the same uniform as I, even the same red engineer braid on his cap. But his skin was the color of light chocolate and the bus driver, a heavy shouldered man hunched over the wheel as if he were permanently shaped to fit his occupation, was glaring at him with an unfriendly expression. "Get on back there," he snarled, "You know whur you s'posed to be!"

Without a word or change of expression, the young man began to push into the crowd, squeezing past the standing passengers who pressed closer to each other to let him pass. I stood there amazed at the absurdity of the scene. Inconvenience for all in order to humiliate one!

The driver turned to me, his closest passenger, as if seeking approval for what he had done. He said, "They know they s'posed to be in the back of the bus."

I blurted, with considerable feeling I think, "But he's an American soldier—in uniform!" The man turned on me a look of such intense hatred I felt my heart thump in anticipation of violence.

He growled, "That don't make no difference!" The bus had started to roll forward so he had to look back to the front, but for the next block or so he kept turning to glare at me as if I were a mortal enemy. I turned my back on him and studied the faces of the crowded passengers. Had any of them heard our exchange? Did they share the driver's feelings about me, the outsider, undoubtedly a damn Yankee, who had expressed aversion to a custom they had never questioned? They were not looking at me. They were tired from a days work, hot and uncomfortable; showing no interest in what had transpired.

Later I fantasized about what I could have done. I could have gone with my fellow soldier to the back of the bus. A still wilder thought: I could have shouted "All soldiers to the back of the bus!" Was I foolish enough to believe that one voice, raised against a custom that was engrained in these people, would have shamed any of them?   Not in that year of 1944. Eleven more years would pass before the famous bus ride of Rosa Parks.

CHAPTER 13

THE TRIP TO EUROPE

It is not true that I was seasick on the Staten Island Ferry. The only connection between that sudden, transient illness and sea-sickness was this: After that disgrace which may not have become as widely known as I believed at the time, I vowed that I would make whatever effort was required, physical or mental, never to be actually seasick. In this I was successful, as I will explain later.

The true story of the ferry incident is as follows. Just before we left Camp Kilmer, New Jersey, I was put in charge of a final cleanup detail in the barracks we had been occupying. The cleanup was redundant,-the departing troops had been required to leave the area immaculate. I and the privates of my detail found only one item—or should I say collection of items—that had to be dealt with. One of the departing soldiers had left a bag of oranges in an otherwise empty footlocker. With no work to do, we simply sat around talking and eating oranges until all were consumed. Within the hour I found myself experiencing waves of nausea as I struggled on board the well-known ferry under the weight of a huge duffel bag containing all my military property. This exertion magnified the malaise that had been induced by overindulgence in acidic oranges. I think I had eaten at least a half dozen. We were jammed together on the deck of the ferry, standing room only, and as soon as the vessel was underway the almost imperceptible rocking caused waves of nausea to sweep over me. I pushed my way to the rail and heaved up into the dark waters of New York Harbor. This inspired whoops of laughter from my comrades. Needless to say my embarrassment was great. Whatever my reputation before that moment—if any—it was now forgotten as I became the only soldier known to have become sea sick on the Staten Island Ferry.

Soon we were marched out onto a dock beside the ship that was to carry us across the sea. The sergeant brought us to a halt then gave the command "at ease." Whereupon we did that which we had become accustomed to doing: We yelled "Huba Huba!" Soldiers of other units nearby seemed to think this was funny. Someone yelled, "They sound like a bunch of ducks quacking!"

Afterr that we filed up a gangplank and down into the lower regions of a Liberty Ship. Bunks were arranged in tiers above one another along narrow aisles. The overall appearance was that of the stacks in a large library, only here instead of bookshelves it was bunks for soldiers, arranged to accommodate the maximum number of men in the allotted space. There was barely room to lie down in a bunk, and the occupant of the bunk overhead was so close that if he turned over in the night a knee or elbow might prod the sleeper below right through the canvass of the bunk above him. In the narrow space that became mine by the luck of the draw, there was an additional problem. The man in the bunk overhead was suffering from an illness that did not improve as the days went by. I believe he was eventually moved to sick bay, and according to later information he was sent back to the USA immediately after arriving in England.

I am sure his condition reflected the nature of the physical examination we had been given just prior to embarkation. Our whole battalion had been lined up in single file and marched past a small group of medical examiners. I never knew what they were looking for. There was certainly not enough time for any kind of actual test, even the taking of temperature. Midway through the examination procedure—if one could call it that—the examiners became aware that another unit, perhaps another whole battalion, was being assembled in line back of ours. At that point the next fifty or so men were ordered to double-time past the doctors. Yes, they actually ran past the medical examiners, presumably to meet some time schedule that had been set up for getting this multitude of men afloat.

There were various stories about how soldiers were examined to see if they were fit for combat. One of these claimed that a cold mirror was held in front of the man's face. If his breath fogged the glass he was deemed fit for duty. While this of course was only a facetious story concocted by a soldier to amuse his comrades, it was a fact that in our case, merely walking or jogging past the examiners was considered evidence that the we were fit to be sent to war.

Our last few days before departure had passed in a rush of activity but now on the crowded troopship we were suddenly men of leisure. The only requirement was that we spend a great deal of time standing in line if we wished to be fed. The chow line started on the crowded, open deck and snaked down into the depth of the ship, passing the entrance to the latrines on the way so that those unfortunates who were suffering from sea sickness could dash out of line and perform their anguished heaving. When they staggered back from the latrine, expended and pale, they were commanded by the merciless sergeant in charge to go up on deck and fall in at the back of the line. Later the rumor spread that some of the afflicted men had not eaten for the whole trip as they were unable to persevere through the long line, and especially past the latrine, without succumbing to the need to engage in violent, presumably unproductive, heaving. This was probably an exaggeration as we were at sea for twelve days. And what about the soldier who had, allegedly, become sea sick on the ferryboat plying the flat waters of New York harbor? Through sheer determination plus the application of a bit of scientific thought about the interaction between visual centers of the brain and semicircular canals in the middle ear, I retained my health and my dignity. Since it's the conflicting signals received by eyes and ears that causes the sickness, I spent a great deal of time on deck staring at the horizon or a distant ship in the convoy and pretending I was swaying deliberately as on a dance floor. Below decks, I kept my eyes closed as much as possible and concentrated on keeping my balance as if I were walking on a tightrope or railroad rail. I was ever ready to explain the theory of my method to any companion in need, but often found myself being glared at by an unbeliever with the chalky face and bleary eyes of the desperately ill. All I know for sure is that the method worked for me not only on this relative smooth, first crossing of the Atlantic but also later on a more stressful crossing of the English Channel on a flat bottomed LST (landing ship for tanks) that was alleged to keep even experienced sailors in a permanent state of malaise. And finally it worked on the return crossing of the Atlantic the following year in very rough weather where the ship tossed so heavily even the happiness of returning home did not prevent widespread sickness.

I might add that the food was scarcely worth the trouble of standing in line. The mashed potatoes were tasteless, presumably prepared from a dry powder which must have come from long dead potatoes. The meat was tough and of a strange color, and the bread smelled moldy.

The trip was long because we were in a convoy of many ships and had to proceed at the speed of the slowest. The convoy consisted of troop ships, cargo ships and many guarding war ships. The ocean seemed covered with ships as far as one could see in every direction. One day an alarm was sounded and crew members dashed through the crowd of soldiers on deck, actually knocking some soldiers down in their furious rush to battle stations. There were explosions in the distance and everyone tried to rush over to the starboard rail to see what was happening. Far away—half way to the horizon—sleek destroyers were racing along, rushing past the larger ships and presumably dropping depth charges. I realized afterwards that this was so much like a scene in a movie I felt no personal association with what was going on. I had no feeling of concern about safety, just an intense interest in the distant action. The only evidence of fear was displayed by one of the sailors who seemed to have fallen in a sort of fit, moaning and shaking uncontrollably. He was being assisted below by two of his companions. They explained to curious soldiers that the man had been on board a ship that was torpedoed on a run to the Russian port of Murmansk. He had never recovered from the trauma of that experience and continued to suffer nervous collapse at the first hint of another attack. I thought it admirable that his companions, tough young sailors, were demonstrating sympathy for his condition. We didn't know about post traumatic stress in those days and I suppose many of the watching soldiers simply concluded the man was a coward.

CHAPTER 14

ARRIVAL IN ENGLAND

I came on deck one morning to find the crowd at the port rail staring at bluffs of a foreign coast. Word passed, "It's the south coast of Ireland." Our plodding convoy moved on through the day and following night and at last we entered a busy port crowded with vessels. We were told we were landing in Bristol but there are several possible landing places near that city and we saw nothing of the city as were marched down the gangplank onto a dock, then immediately loaded on a train for departure to another destination. I noted with amusement that this was the Great Western Railroad—a name reminiscent of the Atchison, Topeka and Santa Fe crossing the vast open spaces of the American southwest. But here the train of the Great Western Railroad raced quickly from town to town through the green countryside of south-west England, its squeaky whistle sounding for frequent road crossings.

We soon arrived at out destination, the railway station in Weston Super Mare. We were marched through the streets of the town to our billet on the grounds of a large house located on a hill. One of our jokers declared the name of the town referred to a female racehorse of unusual speed. Actually it meant "Weston Above the Sea," as we marched up the hill we were greeted by little groups of women who had come out of their houses to watch us pass. One group was singing an amusing song I had not heard before.

> "We don't know where, where, where we're going today.
> We heard the Captain say, we hit the road today.
> We only hope the blinkin' sergeant major knows the way.

The song was rendered in what sounded to me like an Australian dialect: "We dunt know whur, whur, whur we're goin todie." Later, Harry, a scholarly comrade from Temple University, pointed out that there was a gloomy implication here, at least to American ears. "We don't know where we're going to die! But Harry was unusually sensitive to the exact meaning of words. "*Le mot exact*," he would say when talking about his intention to become a writer. He was currently involved in translating a French novel into English.

Marching up the hill we came to our assigned barracks, Quonset huts in the front garden of a large house. Inside the hut, wooden bunk beds were arranged along the walls. These were not a familiar kind of bed for American soldiers. No sheets or blankets were provided. The surface on which we were to sleep was simply a thin sheet of wood, like plywood, with a slight depression, as if the surface had warped downward under the weight of sleeping men. On this we were to place our sleeping bags and whatever we could contrive as a pillow, a folded up jacket for example. Incidentally the air inside the hut had a clammy feeling as if the humidity were very high. This was confirmed in the early morning hours of the next day as I awoke to find big garden snails crawling up the wall beside my bed.

But that first evening was not over for many of the men. Apparently some of my fellow soldiers had perceived something more promising in those groups of women serenading us as we marched up the hill. Where I had seen only patriotic housewives, mostly middle-aged and somewhat dowdy looking by American standards, they had seen the promise of lonely women ready to offer comfort to lonely soldiers. Instead of preparing for bed, they were talking excitedly to one another as they donned clean uniforms and knotted neckties in preparation for a night on the town. Next day they were full of stories about the adventures they had had in this foreign land far from their own wives and families. The most surprising discovery they reported was that the women will do it only while standing up. There was much debate about this. Do they believe they won't become pregnant if they remain standing? Are they influenced by a biblical injunction not to lie with a man who is not their husband? I remember that one tall soldier who had encountered a small woman of generous personality complained of the strain on his knees.

Meanwhile it seemed we were being forced to adjust to all the rigors of English army life. After a night on bare boards, we were introduced to how our hardy allies perform their morning ablutions. Lining up out of doors, facing a sort of trough with many cold water faucets, we were to wash our faces and whatever other areas of our body we were willing to expose to the biting cold of the English Autumn. By the evening of that first day, Yankee ingenuity kicked in and we were heating water for shaving in our steel helmets, placing these makeshift bowls on top of the coal- burning stove which stood in the center of our barracks. A few days later we learned that more extensive bathing, suitable for one who hoped to participate in indoor social activities, was available at a price. The hotels along the beach, war-deprived of most of their vacationer income, were offering baths for a reasonable fee. For a soldier who had not seen a bath tub since leaving home, hot water, scented soap and a thick towel were real luxuries.

As for our army duties, those in charge of Headquarters Company seemed to be desperately searching for busy work. While the line companies of the battalion (Companies A, B, and C) were out in the streets and parks marching to and fro, their sergeants bellowing commands with unusual gusto for the benefit of admiring civilians, Headquarters Company strained to look busy. The motor pool mechanics, confronted by an array of brand new vehicles, pretended to do meaningful work by dissembling some part of a new truck, then putting it back together again. Wheel bearings seemed to be favorite objects for this unnecessary exercise. Even I, the motor pool electrician, unemployed as usual, was tapped one day to dissemble a wheel bearing, remove its grease, then re-grease it and put it back together. The first one was fun if you had nothing else to do. One of my greasy colleagues suggested that I was bucking for promotion. "Promotion?" I snarled. "Since when is electrician to grease monkey a promotion?

Later one of the officers caught me reading a book in the cab of a truck and assigned me to company headquarters to keep the coffee fresh and hot. At the time I preferred to believe this had happened because

I was the only member of the motor pool with clean hands and finger nails. Actually not an unpleasant assignment since it allowed me plenty of time, between pots, for reading. And I should mention, in passing, that preparation of the coffee was a primitive procedure involving no precise measurements of either coffee or water. When the coffee in the pot became low I simply added enough water t o fill it to near the brim (without bothering to remove the old, used grounds) then added what intuition told me was somewhere near the right amount of ground coffee. Then I put the pot back on the electric hot plate and as soon as there was evidence of boiling the new batch of coffee was ready to drink. Usually this resulted in coffee that was too strong but I soon found there were few complaints about this. Weak coffee on the other hand was rejected with disgust. Every few days there was a flurry of physical training activity to keep us fit. Long marches in the country were the preferred activity. Sometimes we were trucked to areas of attractive scenery for these hikes. We suspected that the recon officer was an admirer of the English countryside—of hills decorated by sheep, stone walls and hedgerows, of seaside vistas with waves and screaming gulls, of forests of ancient oaks. He even found a cottage with a thatched roof to march us past. I found these walks in the country interesting and invigorating. We sucked the cold, damp air into our lungs, enjoyed the weak English sunlight on our faces, and stepped out briskly to the cadence count of the sergeant in charge. I think I understand why English soldiers march with an exaggerated strut and swing their arms with unnecessary vigor—its to keep warm.

Word spread that there were nightly dances at a pavilion on the town dock called "The Winter Garden." Arriving there for the first time one evening I was amazed to find the place crowded with college-age girls. More amazing, they *were* college girls. A teachers college had been evacuated from bomb-scarred London to this small resort town that was considered an unlikely target for the *Luftwaffe*. The temporary college campus was a row of resort hotels along the beach. The girls were lively talkers and had plump faces; the latter said to be due to a diet consisting almost exclusively of potatoes. We soon learned that a favorite kind of date for these hungry young women was dinner at a restaurant. They didn't seem to mind that the fare in these establishments invariably involved nothing but potatoes and fish. It soon became evident that one might as well order the special of the day, fish and chips, since these were the only ingredients available.

At another dance, that I seem to remember as a party for headquartes company, we were introduced to the song, "Boomps a Daisy." Everybody sang the simple lyrics and each time they came to the word "Boomps" the women swung their hips sideways and hit their partner a solid blow. Bumping butts was apparently great fun. Everybody yelled and laughed and sang the simple lyrics—Daisy rhymed with lazy and that was about it.

Soon much of my off-duty time was being spent in what one might call a postman's holiday. Mary, whom I met at the Winter Garden, was one of those hearty, out door, English girls who are addicted to long walks, especially on cold, windy days. There wasn't much else to do in war-time Weston although I recall that we went to at least one movie. It was the American film: Home in Indiana. During an idyllic scene of a green countryside with tall hedge rows and fine horses, Mary leaned toward me, hugged my arm and said in a tender voice, "This must be making you terribly homesick." Apparently the movie had rendered me mentally comatose. Instead of taking my cue from this seeming expression of affection I muttered, truthfully, "I've never been in Indiana."   Mary may have been responsible for the fact that I never asked for a pass to visit London. Our company office issued passes for week-end visits to London in spite of the fact that V2 rockets, fired from across the channel, were falling on that city and doing horrific damage. Although the Germans dropped over a thousand V2 s on London during several months starting in September 1944, the area of the city is so vast the chance of one of our soldiers being at ground zero during his short vacation there was very slight. Men returned and told of hearing loud explosions every few hours—usually at a distance. One man claimed there was a double explosion each time one of the rockets fell. This double bang may have been a mystery to Londoners of that time. The idea of a sonic boom, created by the rocket moving through the upper atmosphere faster than the speed of sound was probably known only to the experts. The first test flights of manned supersonic aircraft were soon to come, by Geoffrey De Havilland in England, whose experimental plane apparently disintegrated when it reached a speed of Mach 1, and by Chuck Yeager who survived a first super-sonic flight over the Mojave Desert and became an American hero.

CHAPTER 15

THE BARBER SHOP

I found a barber shop on the quaint English street. I had an important date with Mary for that Friday night and I was determined not to get another of those military haircuts that present a picture of misplaced ears and a preview of baldness in the shaving mirror every morning. The military cut I suspect was introduced for the First World War doughboy, one that would provide fewer hiding places for lice, the common fellow travelers of men engaged in trench wrfare.

The barber was a middle aged chap with one of those gaunt faces that seem to be *de rigueur* for former members of the British armed forces. He greeted me in a reserved, cordial manner , that is to say there was no smile as he rapped out something like come in soldier which I didn't exactly understand but which had the feel of a welcome. There was no one in the single barber chair and the seats for waiting patrons were also vacant. As soon as I was in the chair and properly draped he began to talk after the manner of barbers everywhere. He told me that he had been a soldier in France, in the trenches, for long terrible months in the "first German war." He had been a private in a distinguished British regiment. He had had many harrowing experiences over there—and as he reminisced it became apparent that he had a real antipathy to the British officer class. He said they were Officers only because they were the sons of important people. If papa had a title or a lot of money the son was sure to be made an officer. They were all snobs—never communicated with a common soldier except to dress him down for some trivial or imaginary shortcoming, or to shout an order. He declared most officers have no imagination and no new ideas. The generals were the worst—they were forever repeating the tactics of former wars. Napoleon won his battles by sending hordes of man charging toward the enemy line in the face of musket fire. This worked because a man with a musket could fire only three rounds in a minute---four if he was a Prussian, or so it was claimed by Prussians of course. Furthermore, in the old days, muskets were not aimed deliberately at individual enemies—they were simply leveled and fired on command. This was an agreeable form of battle for officers. Seated high up on their big horses they were above the line of fire and seldom stopped bullets except with their legs. In the first German war the same strategy was used against enemies armed with machine guns. The generals had ordered great masses of men to charge the enemy lines. After such a mindless charge had failed with the slaughter of thousands of men, the generals could think of only one solution: send in more men the next time. Inspired by his tale of officer folly I recited the story of Pickett's charge at Getysburg where thousands of rebel soldiers charged across almost a mile of open ground against a more numerous federal Army equipped with abundant cannons and the first repeating rifles used in war. So what did military planners learn between 1863 and 1914? Apparently not much.

As the barber talked, he seemed to be doing a meticulous job on my hair. I was thinking here is a man who takes pride in his work and is only satisfied with perfection. But perhaps he was only enjoying the conversation and wanted to prolong it. The flow of words stopped as the door opened and our own picturesque Captain T. entered. Tall, slim, in immaculately pressed uniform and shiny shoes, he sported an Errol Flynn mustache and an unauthorized air-corps style hat with a gold eagle rampant above the bill. Only his swagger stick was missing. At least he had the good taste not to carry it on an English street—or maybe he had misplaced it.

I was now confronted with a military courtesy dilemma. Should I spring from my chair, cone to attention in my flowing barber's drapery and give a snappy salute? That seemed a bit much, so I just sat there, hoping for the best, prepared to greet him politely if he acknowledged my existence. He didn't.

Fortunately he had removed his hat as he came through the door and I seemed to remember, from a novel or the movies, that you don't salute an officer if he is uncovered. He sat down, picked up the newspaper from an adjacent chair and began to peruse the front page. Soon he was frowning unhappily. No wonder. English newspapers were criticizing the performance of the American army in the Ardennes.

American news sources were praising the heroic stand of our troops against the surprise German offensive in what was soon to be called the battle of the bulge. They were charmed by the story of how our General McAuliffe had responded to the German demand for surrender with a single expletive, misquoted by the squeamish newspapers of the time as "Nuts!" No soldier could understand why the general would emit that mild exclamation. Many believed that what he actually said was the Anglo- Saxon word for excrement.

The English view of the situation in the battle was biased, it being the common opinion that if British troops under their much adored Monty—General Bernard Montgomery—had been manning the front in the Ardennes, the Germans would have been stopped cold with devastating losses. Editorials were grumbling that Eisenhower had not allowed a proper role for "Monty" and were even reviving memories of the disaster at Kasserine Pass, in Tunisia, where in February of nineteen forty three, inexperienced American troops had been sent into battle against the war-hardened veterans of Rommel's Afrika Corps with disastrous results.

Captain T. put the paper down, and sat glowering at the wall for a few minutes, then turned his attention to me. He said, "Edmonds , that's a gigolo haircut. You should be getting a military cut".

The barber made a sound in his throat like a bull dog that has just spotted the neighbor's cat sneaking into the yard. There was a pause as I scrambled for a suitable and permissible reply. Finally I asked, "Sir, is that an order or a suggestion?"

He answered promptly, "A suggestion. It's no skin off my butt if you get gigged for having the longest hair in the company a few weeks from now. There won't be any barber shops where were going."

End of conversation. Silence reigned, except for the now vigorous snipping of the scissors. I began to fear for my ears. When the barber removed the apron, I stood up, replaced my cap and adjusted its angle carefully. I paid and tipped the barber, and received a comradely thank you. I about faced smartly and—now that I was in proper uniform again—gave the captain a salute and said "Good day, Sir." His right hand rose, not exactly an acknowledgment of my salute, more like a gesture of dismissal.

I left, looking forward to seeing him again—to see just how bad his haircut would be—and I sincerely hoped he would ask the barber to trim his mustache.

CHAPTER 16

CROSSING THE CHANNEL

On the last day of December, 1944, we finally arrived in France. We had only one of the hardships of those earlier heroes who had crossed the channel on D day: sea sickness. A huge LST, Landing Ship for Tanks, carried us across the channel from Southampton. This alleged ship, in form a huge steel box, pitched and swayed on the channel waves with erratic motions few human nervous systems could adapt to. Men huddled in their bunks pondering the meaning of human misery, or crouched on the steel deck outside the head, strategically positioned for the next bout of vomiting. Curiously, I seemed to be the only army man on board untouched by this almost universal malady. In early evening, Spode caught me in the act of staring cheerfully over the rail. Actually I was peering at the horizon in the so far successful technique of avoiding motion sickness by watching the only stable reference point in my field of view and trying to fool my balancing mechanism into thinking I was deliberately producing the erratic motions to which it was being subjected.

"Follow me," he commanded, sounding like the traditional, expendable lieutenant leading his men into battle. He led me down to the ships galley and actually paused long enough to explain that, as a matter of courtesy, the army was to provide one helper for the navy staff that was there to serve hot coffee to officers on night duty. For a horrified moment I visualized myself on KP duty, washing dishes at a sink where the hot water was surging in waves from the ships motion. Surely the depression invoked by such menial labor while confined below decks would bring on a bout of sea sickness, but the kindly young black man who had been manning the station alone until my arrival, assured me at once that I was there in a purely symbolic role. "Just make yourself at home and have some coffee," was the way he put it.

Strangely, confined there below decks, in a pitching, swaying box of a galley, I remained free of the obnoxious symptoms that were afflicting my comrades. I wondered if I had, by now, trained my balancing machinery to accept sickening motions without protest. Few officers, either Navy or Army, came by for coffee. "Most of them are seasick," my new colleague explained. He said the vessel, if you could call it that, had made its maiden voyage across the Atlantic to a landing in North Africa and that the "Old Man", which supposedly meant the captian, had been seasick all the way. I reflected that, considering the status of black sailors in the U S navy, the term "Old Massa" might be more appropriate, but I didn't know him well enough to attempt a joke reflecting his ethnic background. I spent much of the night in conversation with him, dozing off a few times in a chair provided for my comfort. He told me proudly of his English girl friend and showed me her picture. It seemed he was ready to adopt the naval tradition of a girl in every port but so far he had been able to explore only one port, Southampton. The girl was white and carrying an infant that was so swathed against the cold I could not note its skin color.

The long night finally passed and relief for my seasick companions came quickly as we passed from the turbulent waves of the channel into the smooth water of the marshland at the mouth of the Seine. We went on deck where the bracing air of a fine winter day restored one and all to health. We were served a hearty navy breakfast and spent a guiltless day of leisure watching the French countryside slide by as we cruised up the Seine. This was about as good as life ever got in the army.

Finally the soaring mass of Rouen Cathedral rose above the horizon marking the destination of our cruise. In late afternoon the LST nuzzled up to a sloping embankment just as it had been designed to do on an enemy beach. Those of us who had no task assigned filed ashore and became spectators of the unloading of the trucks, jeeps, and other rolling stock carried on the huge vehicle deck. The LST towered above us now, looking even more ungainly than when we first saw it at the dock in Southampton. Its huge bow ramp was down and the engines of trucks and other vehicles were beginning to roar in its dark interior.

The master sergeant was in his glory. He was pacing and posing on the shore right where the vehicles would come out, ready to direct the drivers. When the first truck came rolling out into the daylight he yelled and gestured as if he were directing troops in battle. The driver, with the insouciance of a man who is performing a familiar task, ignored him. The other drivers had only to follow the truck ahead, but the master sergeant continued to yell at each as he passed. Farther up the street, a staff sergeant of Italian-American ethnicity was standing. He greeted each driver with a casual flip of his hand, indicating a turn to the left. He grinned at some of the drivers as they approached and one of them yelled at him, "Hey, Roberto Bambino! They finally gave you a job you can do!"

The sergeant called back, "Yeah, Tony, too bad they can't do the same for you."

In what other army in the world would Staff Sergeant and Corporal banter in this manner under the eyes of their officers?

It was dusk when the unloading was finished. We were marched deeper into the blacked-out city. The great bulk of the damaged cathedral loomed not far away like a ghost from another age. Our destination was an army transient mess hall, a place where large numbers of troops on the move could be provided with hot meals. The place was redolent with the odor of cooking food. Long tables were aligned in the middle of the building and a milling throng of soldiers was arriving, eating and leaving. Some men were in the filthy uniforms of infantry just back from the front, some were in new uniforms with clean packs on their backs—replacements being sent to the front to take the place of men wounded or killed in battle. Off to one side religious services were underway. The catholic chaplain had a makeshift alter of two foot lockers, one on top of the other, draped with a white alter cloth. I was surprised to see one of our toughest and loudest sergeants kneeling before the alter, taking communion. Protestant ministers were holding forth in their chosen locations but most of the men were in a rush to get to the serving line. I passed down the row of servers and received a generous portion of roast beef, mashed potatoes with brown gravy, and a thick slice of bread. I found a seat next to Harry at one of the tables.

Some of out headquarters clerks and medics were seated on the other side of the table facing us. These were men who were usually cleanly shaved, neatly combed and shod in clean shoes. Now they were dressed in grubby fatigues, unshaved and had haggard unsmiling faces. One who rose to seek a second helping, displayed muddy shoes as he waked away. A plump-faced medic, noted for his cheery disposition and repertoire of dirty jokes, actually glared across the table at us, as if resentful of some aspect of our appearance. He demanded to know, "How did you guys get across the channel?"

Harry described the seasick misery of our channel crossing and the pleasure of our cruise up the Seine. We were surprised at the anger this aroused on the other side of the table. The explanation for this came in fragmentary accounts, biased by their obvious exhaustion, and resentment of how they had been treated. At the dock in Southampton all the men not involved with the motorized equipment had been ordered on board an ancient British freighter with rusty sides and cluttered decks. Their ship was manned by little brown men who spoke no English. A ship's officer, white, but looking more like a pirate than a British sea captain, had described the crew as sepoys, a term usually applied to East Indian troops serving under British officers. They seemed like cheerful little fellows and our men found them amusing to watch, at first. But soon their hygienic customs began to inspire surprise. Each man carried a little bowl hooked onto his belt which he used for sanitary purposes. After urinating in the bowl he carefully emptied it on the lee side of the ship then wiped it out with a dirty rag before hanging it, and the rag, again on his belt. When dinnertime arrived, large pots of stew, composed of unknown ingredients, were wheeled out on deck and our men lined up, mess gear in hand, expecting to be served as usual by chefs equipped with serving spoons. But no, they were expected to serve themselves by dipping the aluminum bowls of their mess kits into the stew. This seemed a minor deviation in chow line procedure until several men at the head of the line made the same observation and had the same thought. A small cluster of the sepoys were sitting on the deck, eating their stew from those same little bowls that had been used for another purpose earlier. Had they dipped those bowls in the stew? The chow line broke up amidst a chorus of angry exclamations and curses. There was no dinner that night for the fastidious. Hungry soldiers went their beds, sleeping bags on hard steel decks, cursing the quaint customs of the British navy.

Morning brought no respite from their ordeal. They were ordered to leave the ship far down-stream from Rouen. Apparently the ancient freighter had to have deeper water than our flat bottomed LST. They ate a makeshift breakfast of emergency rations, then were marched away over the French countryside, trudging on and on for hours, past fields and through villages, before the cathedral appeared on the horizon. It was mid afternoon when they arrived at the transient dining room. They ate a late lunch, then sprawled on the winter-dead grass of a nearby park and slept the sleep of the exhausted until dinnertime.

Now we were all together again—all the men of headquarters company—so of course we were all assumed to be equally ready to travel on. Well-rested technicians from the motor pool, sore-footed clerks and medics—all to be treated the same by the firm but fare Army. We marched or limped, according to our current condition, a quarter mile or so across town to where the vehicles were parked. Everyone was ordered onto the troop carriers, trucks with the usual hard benches along each side of the bed. But we members of the motor pool all had the same idea—as our drivers dashed to their assigned trucks, we went with them and found comfortable seating in the cabs beside them. I found a place in the truck of a driver I didn't know. He was a new man in the outfit and a private, so he accepted me into the vacant seat without greeting or comment.

The vehicles were assembled into a convoy as they left the parking area. The recon officer's jeep led the way, followed by the heavy equipment, tank recovery wreakers, bulldozers on long flatbed trailers, then the trucks carrying cargo and troops. Soon we were out of the city and rolling along a dark highway with only the dim blackout lights of the vehicle ahead showing the way. I asked the driver if he knew where we were going. He said he had been ordered to follow the truck ahead, nothing else.   Hope for a cot in a transient camp faded as we went on and on through the darkness.

I hope I thought with sympathy of those men with the sore feet— exhausted by a day of walking across the French countryside, now crammed together on the hard seats of the troop carriers. But probably

I didn't give them a thought. A soldier grabs whatever comfort falls to him, knowing he will pay for it later with discomfort, or worse.

CHAPTER 17

A NIGHT TO REMEMBER

When I awoke I was sitting upright on the right hand seat of the truck. It seemed to me I was held in this position by the heavy engineers' mackinaw and the layers of clothing under it as if I were in a body cast. The convoy was still rolling along a narrow, paved highway; trucks with their faint blackout lights in ghostly procession. I looked over at the driver, a dark silhouette against the faint starlight of the window. Only his big hands on the steering wheel, moving from time to time, proclaimed his humanity. I said, "Are we driving all night?"

He was slow to answer. Maybe he was offended by my saying "We." Finally he growled, "No sweat for you, Mac. You been sleepin like uh tomcat after a busy night."

I felt guilty. There was no way I could help with the driving. I didn't have a driver's specialist number. My civilian driver's license had no status here. So I just shifted into a more comfortable position and gazed out at the passing landscape. It was a surreal scene in black and white. The fields were dusted by a thin coating of new snow. The ridges of the furrows were black lines reaching off into the darkness. From time to time a row of pollarded trees appeared beside the road, the tops of their trunks were swollen where new limbs had been removed year after year. Their shape suggested a tall black mushroom with a white cap of snow. A road sign came into view, "Arras, 60 KM" Soon another sign appeared, at a crossroad, It pointed to the left "Dieppe." These were towns remembered from the headlines of 1940 when Hitler's panzers roared across northern France, sweeping remnants of the French army and most of the British forces into the pocket around Dunkirk. From the signs I knew we were headed east and if the convoy was to travel all night we must be urgently needed. An officer had said, "They don't need engineers. They need more men with rifles."

Soon the whole line of trucks swung over to the right side of the road and came to a stop. The army provided breaks for tired drivers--- not out of kindness but to reduce the accident rate. I stepped down into a shallow ditch, my feet sinking into a cushion of mingled grass and snow. A small group of men soon gathered just down the line. I moved to join them. Maybe someone knew something about our destination. As I approached them, one of the men raised his hands to his face and a cigarette lighter flared for a moment. In the light his face was bony and harsh—the face of a man older than the typical soldier. It was Carl, the hard rock miner from Colorado, our top demolitions man, known for the skill with which he handled dangerous explosives and his disdain for army rules. From up the line of trucks a commanding voice shouted: "Douse that light!"

While the pale blue blackout lights on the trucks could be seen for only a hundred yards or so, the red glow of a cigarette could be seen, so it was said, by a pilot flying high overhead.

Another voice, louder and nearer, echoed the command, embellishing it with an obscenity. Carl cupped his hands around the cigarette to conceal it. But he seemed to be taking a long, satisfying drag for a red glow illuminated his face. One of the soldiers in the group said, "Put the damned thing out, you're gonna get us all in trouble." Carl threw the cigarette across the ditch. It flew in a shower of sparks to be quenched in the snow. The officer yelled again, "Get that man's name!"

Someone was hurrying along the ditch from the other direction, probably the non-com who had yelled earlier. I decided not to join that group. I stepped between two trucks and out into the left side of the road. The drivers were there, stalking up and down, waving their arms, stamping their feet, in an effort to revive circulation. I joined them in this endeavor, stamping and stretching my arms. Drivers were subject to the condition called trench foot. Men got it in the First World War from standing in the cold water of trenches. In this war truck drivers got it from sleeping in the cabs of their trucks with their feet against the cold steel floor.

Soon there was a shouted command, "Mount up." I wondered if that officer was a transfer from the cavalry.

As I started to return to my seat in the truck I had a sudden inspiration. When we had been loading up in Rouen I had noticed that the truck in which I found a vacant seat was loaded with duffel bags. These were the large, cylindrical canvas bags in which each soldier carried his extra uniforms, socks, underwear and so forth. As I passed back of the truck I reached into the darkness of the cargo space and reassured myself the bags were there. I quickly placed my rifle and helmet inside, then vaulted up over the tailgate and crawled forward over the piled up bags. I found a depression to my liking and squirmed into a sort of nest, with bags underneath me, a higher one for a pillow and a place for my cold feet under another. It was the best bed I had occupied for a long time. The truck moved forward with a soothing hum and gentle bounces. I fell asleep at once.

I was awakened by the beam of a flashlight assaulting my eyelids. The truck had stopped. Someone was back there looking in. A voice that I recognized—one that I didn't want to hear—called out, "Who's in there?" It was Mr. Spode. He played the flashlight beam around the interior of the cargo space, found the helmet liner with my name stenciled on the front and called out , almost jovially, "Edmonds, come out of there. Bring your rifle and steel helmet."

I crawled to the opening, sure that Spode was rousting me out of my bed simply because he couldn't bear to see a soldier sleeping in such comfort, but as my mind cleared I registered the second part of his command. "Bring your rifle and helmet." That seemed to hint at duty to be performed. I slid out and down to the ground feet first. The surface of the road was icy. I would have fallen if I had not been clutching the upper edge of the tailgate with both gloved hands. Yes, I had been sleeping with my gloves on, also a wool cap. I retrieved my rifle and held it between my legs while I struggled to meld the steel helmet, its fiber glass liner and the wool cap into one protective structure.

Spode said, "Hurry up. Get in the jeep." The jeep, its engine idling, was facing back down the line of trucks toward the rear of the convoy. Spode had already mounted into the driver's seat. I dashed to the other side of the jeep and sprang up into the right hand front seat. This was the reverse of the usual seating arrangement. Ordinarily, officers did not drive. It was said an officer who wrecked a vehicle would be expected to pay for it out of his salary. But Spode was a warrant officer—that curious hybrid, addressed as mister, who is above all enlisted men but below commissioned officers. Perhaps the rule didn't apply to him. I knew he had been a manager of a taxi company. Perhaps he had worked up from taxi driver. He drove like one now. The speed limit for army vehicles was thirty-five miles per hour, but I think Spode had the accelerator pressed against the floor. The wind came around and over the sparse windshield in a freezing blast. I was tempted to put my gloved hands over my cheeks and nose but I was sure Spode would consider that unmilitary behavior. Fortunately we did not have far to go; we soon came to a cross road. Spode slowed at the last possible moment and skillfully swung the jeep into a U-turn which finished with a sidewise skid.

He said, "Get out." I did. He leaned toward me and in a loud voice, as if he were talking to a mentally defective person or a willful child, said, "Guard this intersection. Stop all traffic going that way." He pointed down the road from which we had come. "Tell them a flatbed trailer is jackknifed across the road. Road will be blocked for several hours."

He was off with a howling engine. The spin of the rear wheels sprayed me with icy slush from the road. I stood there surveying the dark, desolate scene. The foreign landscape stretched away in every direction with no evidence of life. If there were houses between me and the horizon they were totally blacked out. I suddenly felt more alone than I had ever been. There was an eerie unreality about the whole situation and I soon became a victim of nagging unease. First there was the concern that Spode would forget to come back for me. None of us trusted Spode to do the right thing for the soldiers under him. Then I began to think about the rumors I had heard that the Germans were parachuting spies back of our lines—intruders dressed in American uniforms and trained to speak English with an American accent. With growing alarm I remembered that their mission was said to be the disruption of army traffic by misdirecting drivers at road crossings. Soon I had worked out in my imagination a complete scenario of what was likely to happen. I would be interrogated on the spot by a tense and trigger-happy officer whose attitude had been hardened by combat. The interview would go like this: "O.K. Soldier, if you're for real, name the teams in the world series, for the last five years. Ah, Ha! You can't do it, can you? Sergeant, take this kraut spy out into the field there and shoot him.' What an ignominious end: to die wishing I had been an avid sports fan!

I was pacing up and down, not because it was my military duty to do so but because my feet were numb with cold. After a while I became aware of a strange phenomenon taking place to the east: A continuous flickering of light low down in the sky along the horizon. The country was flat and the night was clear so the display could be at a great distance. It reminded me of the mysterious "heat lightning" of our western prairies— actually a thunder storm over the horizon, to far away to be heard. But this was not lightning. With a feeling of awe I realized I was seeing the front. The flickering lights were the muzzle flashes of big guns. As I watched, bursts of light appeared higher in the sky—flack, anti-aircraft shells, exploding above the front. Was this the battle that we were being rushed to so urgently that our battalion must travel all night?

I was so intent on the light show that I didn't see the bicycle until it was almost entering the intersection. A slim figure, probably male, was hunched over the handle bars. He seemed to be going slower and slower, as if reluctant to pass the mysterious soldier guarding the crossroad. His bicycle was wobbling now, threatening to fall over. I gestured to him to come on, waving him past. I used my school-boy French to wish him a good evening. He responded with a choking sound, almost a moan. After he passed me, he rose up into the stance of a racer in the Tour de France. His rear wheel actually spun on the icy surface as he accelerated. He fled down the road to the south and vanished into the darkness.

I went back to pacing. Time passed slowly. It seemed like several hours before a strange jeep came up the road from the south. It headed right toward me, then came to a stop so close I stepped back to avoid a wheel over my toes. It had a canvas top and side curtains, with an opening beside the driver. He was sitting right there in front of me, his broad face barely visible in the darkness, but what was visible was the barrel of a handgun pointed right at my navel, range about four inches. The gun would not have bothered me—it was to be expected under the circumstances—but then the driver spoke, in a deep guttural voice, "Heil Hitler!"

I froze. An icy wave seemed to engulf me. I am sure I stopped breathing—perhaps my heart paused too. My stomach seemed to be trying to crawl out of the path of the bullet. A flashlight beam played on my stricken face and there was a cruel chuckle from inside the jeep. The driver spoke again, this time a grits and molasses voice from somewhere south "Jest whut the hail you doin out heah all by yousef, Kid?

My heart began to beat again. I took a few deep breaths. I then started to recite the message which Spode had instructed me to deliver. When I began my voice was strained and peculiar but when I got to the part about the road being blocked I was surprised at the anger in my own voice.

Another voice from the darkness inside the jeep said, "Let's check that out". The driver gunned the engine, surged forward, circling to take the road to the east. As the jeep turned I saw for the first time the white, stenciled letters on its side: MP (Military police).

For some unexplainable reason that was the final straw. My rage exploded into tantrum mode. I yelled at the departing jeep an army-learned obscenity so vile it had never passed my lips before, proclaiming to the empty land and the night sky that this driver had an incestuous relationship with his own mother. Fortunately, the jeep engine was howling in acceleration and the tire chains were chattering fiercely on the icy surface. I suppose they didn't understand me, or if they did they were having a god laugh at my reaction. I stomped back and forth across the intersection, my rage gradually cooling to the point where I began to notice the numbness of my feet again.

Some time after that another jeep came down the road from the east. It was open to the night sky and the driver had the size and shape of Spode. He pulled up beside me and said, "get in.'

He said not another work as he drove, again generating a freezing wind. This time I pressed my gloved hands to my cheeks and nose; I didn't care now what Spode thought. But in what could have been interpreted as an act of kindness he delivered me to the rear of the same truck from which he had extracted me. As I got out I felt an urge to say, "Happy New Year, Sir." But I kept silent, knowing he would interpret it as sarcasm.

I climbed back into the truck, found my nest among the duffle bags and wriggled into a comfortable position. I heard a distant voice shout, "The guards are in." There was a cacophony of starting and revving engines. My mobile bedroom began to roll again.

I was curious now about how long I had been out—or rather, how much time was left for sleeping. I dug down through the layers of cloth around my wrist and brought the luminous dial of my army watch into view. To my surprise it was only a few minutes after midnight. It was now New Years day, 1945.

CHAPTER 18

TRAVELS IN FRANCE

Dawn found us stopped along the road beside a bare field dusted with snow and an orchard of winter-bare apple trees. We had a cold breakfast except for hot coffee which our valiant cooks somehow managed to deliver. A six-man tent had appeared in the field and was decorated with a red cross proclaiming the medical staff was ready for business. The business was provided by a line up of soldiers seeking medical attention, mostly, I supposed, for blistered feet. I recognized several of the long distance hikers who had crossed the channel in the ship of the unsanitary sepoys. An order came from somewhere for us to pair off and set up two-man tents—pup tents, in preparation for a stay of at least through the next night. I was paired with Earl Stroud for this. We spread or raincoats on the ground to form a "ground cloth." Then snapped our "shelter halves" together to form the tent. Sleeping bags were unrolled inside the tent on the raincoats.

After we had finished this assignment it seemed there was no further planned activity so, left to our own resources, with no commissioned officers in sight, we set about exploring our surroundings. Some of the men, having heard that cider was available, set out toward the nearby farms, hoping fermented apple juice would slack their thirst for a more potent drink. I joined a group that was planning to hike up the road to a village, some roof tops and a church steeple showing the way. As we were entering the town we saw an elderly man emptying his bladder against a stone wall in full view of the people in the street. This performance, though quite amusing to American soldiers, attracted not a glance from the French passersby. Another scene that seemed noteworthy to us: A small group of school children, carrying books and bag lunches were passing a house from which a woman came out and called to them. They paused to see what she wanted and immediately the little boys snatched off their caps in a show of respect. In the village we found a store where we could buy bread and cheese. Since we had no French money we offered cigarettes as a medium of exchange. This worked well; in that village cigarettes were more precious than food!

At dinner time some of the men had managed to build fires. Where they had obtained the firewood in that neatly groomed countryside I could not imagine and thought it better not to ask. The cooks had disappeared, called to take care of the officers we suspected, so we were on our own to prepare emergency rations for the meal. This consisted of canned food in small individual cans. . There was some variety to this food but frankfurters and beans was every ones favorite. We punched holes in the tops of the cans to allow stem to escape, then put them on or as near as possible to the fire. Soon the cans began to sputter, juices oozing out of the steam holes and filling the air with a pleasant aroma. Some of the men were starting to retrieve their cans when there was a sudden, loud explosion in the fire. I had the fleeting thought that a grenade had exploded in our midst but an instant later I was wiping beans and sauce from my face and uniform and joining in the mingled exclamations, curses and laughter as we realized one of the cans had exploded, spraying everyone with its contents. Someone expressed the question that was on everyone's mind: Who is the dummy that didn't punch a steam hole in his can? This became a puzzle after each man extracted his can from the fire and the number of properly punched cans matched the number of men present. Then Joe Bosco (The name is fictitious) came strolling on the scene and started complaining: "Where's my can? I put a can on the fire right here and now it's gone. Who got my can?

To his surprise, this brought an outpouring of verbal abuse with a common theme: "You Screw-up! Don't you know you're supposed to punch the can before you put it in the fire? Joe did a hasty retreat, and we noted that he was going toward the supply tent, presumably in hope of another can of frankfurters and beans.

Spode had appeared before dusk and had promptly set a few men to work erecting a small tent for himself. His tent was in the orchard adjacent to the field so he was somewhat aloof from the common soldiers he was there to supervise. When night came some men nearest his tent were astonished to see that he had donned pajamas before going to bed. Astonished is the right word; no enlisted man in the army ever wore pajamas. The rest of us, in our little tents, had gone to bed fully clothed. In discussing this later we speculated that the officers, comfortable in a French house or inn, might be sleeping in pajamas, and warrant officer Spode was trying to maintain the same high standards even though he had been sent out into the cold to sleep with the enlisted men. In any case he must have had a cold night. Next day he selected a crew to go with a truck to one of the nearby farms where he obtained a large load of straw. When the truck arrived back at our field it was parked near the orchard. We thought the straw was for out tents. We were anticipating soft beds of straw protecting us from the cold ground. For once we felt real gratitude toward Spode. But soon he selected another group of workers and directed them to unload the straw and pile it around and over his tent. More was stacked in front of the tent door to shield it from the wind. This was seen by all as a blatant act of selfishness. Actually, I think he was expressing his resentment at not being allowed to share the comforts of the commissioned officers. He didn't care what we, his lowly followers, thought.

On the sixth of January we left that location near the little village of Le Forges and moved off toward the East and South. Current accounts of the war say that Eisenhower had made the decision that only veteran troops, those hardened by the fighting that had preceded the "Bulge," were to be used to drive the Germans back from the Ardennes. It was probably his aim to destroy completely the mass of enemy troops and their remaining equipment that had been assembled to launch an offensive in the West.

My memories of France that winter are like unrelated pictures from an album or a child's picture book. There were days spent just trying to stay warm. We kept fires burning in empty metal barrels and clustered around them holding out our hands to the heat. In the forest of the Ardennes we pushed trucks up icy hills dodging the flying slush from their spinning wheels. One night the whole motor pool slept upstairs in a French farm house, our sleeping bags side by side covering the floors in four rooms. The house had an indoor toilet consisting of a room with a hole in the middle of the floor. The walls of the stairway were white with something like a lime whitewash. The stairway was so narrow it was difficult to go up or down without brushing against the walls. I think we wiped most of the whitewash off onto the sleeves of our jackets the first day. It was in that house that I lost my razor and my gloves. I wrote a letter home asking that another razor be sent to me but the officer-censor who read the letter had a new razor delivered into my hands by a courier the next day. I was not able to thank him as the identity of officers who censored letters was a well kept secret. Surely for a conscientious officer, reading the private letters of men they knew and saw every day must have seemed like a shameful intrusion of privacy. But of course there was a common excuse: They were following orders.

Always we could hear the sound of the guns. In retrospect, it seems the whole first part of January was a time of simply existing without knowledge of what was going on in the real war—the one that was producing that distant thunder that we head every day. Not until much later did I lean that the Germans had launched the second phase of the "Battle of the Bulge," an operation they called "Nordwind." This was in Alsace, involving the city of Strassbourg where our own seventh army and the Free French forces were holding a long stretch of the front. It was even said that the Germans were trying to take advantage of the fact that Patton's third army, the armored force that they feared most, had gone north to help destroy the bulge. The seventh army was said to be rushing every available man to that front. While our "forgotten battallion" was called upon to do nothing, thousands of American and French troops were being killed and injured, the whole seventh army was being frenziedly reinforced, and the allied armies were in serious risk of being driven apart both physically and psychologically. The later because Eisenhower wanted to draw troops back from Strasbourg in order to straighten the lines, but De Gaulle, though he was nominally under Eisenhower's command, refused, vowing Frenchmen would fight to the death rather then give up that symbolic city even for a few days. The Germans threw what was left of their air force into the battle and this was a bad decision for them. I suppose it was another suicidal directive from Hitler. Surely Herman Goering would not have wanted his beloved Luftwaffe to be destroyed as a futile gesture of defiance against the superior American Army Air Corps which now controlled the skies over France.

Somewhere we rode past an airfield where the huge American fighter planes, the Republic Thunderbolts, were taking off on missions over Germany. American airplane designers, it seemed, were extravagantly providing different kinds of war planes, ranging from large fighters like the thunderbolts to those with twin fuselages like the Lockheed P38. The production of bombers was even more impressive with our factories turning out thousands of B24's (Over eighteen thousand, according to Wikipedia) to hundreds of giant B 17's and finally the even bigger B29's, like the Enola Gay, the plane that dropped the nuclear bomb on Hiroshina.. The awesome productive power of American industry may have peaked during these first months of 1945.

At last our line companies were thrown into Action. Near the Saar River, the men of Headquarters Company spent a sleepless night loading assault boats on trailers in preparation for crossing the river. At midnight A, B and C companies of our battalion manned the boats, ferrying infantry across the Saar. American infantrymen swarmed from the boats onto the east bank of the river to find the Germans had fled. No shots were fired that night.

We moved on south. At Bar Le Duc we were billeted in a hotel. We slept on soft beds under duvets. Men joked that they couldn't sleep on the beds. They claimed they had to put their sleeping bags on the floor—it was more like the hard, frozen ground they had become accustomed to. I believe it was in Bar Le Duc that a half dozen of us went into an expensive Restaurant and ordered dinner. The waiters were in formal attire, the French patrons were evidently of that social class that was surviving the war without any serious sacrifice of luxuries and the food was truly exotic fare for army men who had not tasted anything better than frankfurters and beans for a long time. If we felt out of place with our dirty uniforms, unkempt, unwashed hair and with steel helmets and guns stashed beside our chairs, it didn't interfere with our appetites. I cannot recall what or how I ordered from the unfamiliar menu but I remember my wine was *rouge*. I believe our salaries were being paid in French Francs at that time so there was no difficulty with the check. I doubt that we tipped correctly.

Near Strasbourg we were sent into a hospital to use the shower room. A hot shower was an incredible luxury. We joked later that we stayed in the showers until we were dragged out. While waiting in the area we had conversations with convalescent soldiers. One man was bitter that his division, new soldiers fresh from the training camps of Texas, had been ordered to assault the German line against intense machine gun fire. He told us Americans were slaughtered in that battle. He said, with the outcome of the war already certain the Americans lives were sacrificed just to get the war over with a few days earlier.

The radio news casters were jubilant about the same battle— "Green troops, newly trained, from the camps of Arkansas and Texas, have driven the experienced Germans from their last stand west of the Rhine." This was called the battle of the Comar Pocket.   Another man in the hospital described how anti-aircraft searchlights were innovatively used to blind the enemy soldiers. I expressed surprise that the lights were not simply shot out, but he declared the Germans couldn't tell how far away the lights were. It's like having the sun in your eyes, he said, you couldn't sight a gun at the sun without being blinded and facing the beam from an eight hundred million candlepower searchlight is pretty much the same.

By the end of January "North Wind" was finished, the Germans had finally been cleared from the land of France and our battalion was stalled again, camping beside the wall of an ancient fort at Epinal. I remember camping beside an ancient wall the stones of which were so weathered they seemed to blend into what looked like a natural stony bluff. I t was here that the staff sergeant who had taken the job I was training for in Arkansas met the most important challenge of his career. On our arrival at this camp site he was ordered to construct a latrine for the officers. This required a pit over which the facility would be built. He first attempted to do this with a crew of men wielding picks and shovels, but the surface they were attacking was so hard their progress was distressingly slow—especially for the officers who were waiting to use it. He finally requested help from the demolitions men and they proceeded to blow a hole in the stony surface—an impressive explosion that left men wondering if a bomb had dropped in our midst. After the blast it could be seen that the surface on which the pick and shovel detail had toiled for futile hours was actually a pavement of large stone blocks, part of the structure of the ancient fort, probably the paving of a courtyard. Rumor had it that the Mechanic Foreman, a staff sergeant when the work began, was reduced in grade. (Fewer stripes for his sleeves.) But I did not actually witness this. Perhaps the rumor stemmed from wishful thinking by the exhausted men who had been wielding the picks and shovels.

Toward the beginning of February we moved to Saint Avold. This little city had been an important communication center for the German forces occupying Lorraine. Evidently, the house where Headquarters' Company was billeted had been used by German troops for the same purpose. The upstairs room where we found sleeping quarters was equipped with double deck bunk beds. I remember this clearly because I was in such a bed when we awoke one morning to hear shells dropping on the town. There was a series of explosions not far away and one soldier, one of those know-it-all types ever ready to display his knowledge, announced the sound came from our own guns. He elaborated on this, describing the caliber of the guns and telling where they were located at the edge of town. Reassured by this, we lay there relaxed, listening to the roar of explosions for several minutes. Suddenly there was an explosion so close the whole house shook and tiles slid down the roof, rattling noisily right over our heads. We rolled out of bed and headed down the stairs to see if there was a basement or cellar where we could take shelter. There was none, but the shelling soon stopped as suddenly as it had begun. The town was shelled again the next day but most of the shells fell near our artillery sites on the outskirts of the town. Rumor had it that one or two men were killed by that barrage. Later, after we moved to another town nearby, we heard that St Avold was bombed by German planes only a day or two after our departure.

We were having occasional interactions with French civilians during this time, mostly of a casual nature. At the motor pool in St. Avold, an elderly woman dropped in to the office every day and stayed until we fed her. One day a man stoped me on the street to correct what he saw as a threat to my uniform. I had carelessly thrust a pencil into my shirt pocket and he was disturbed that it was point down. He reached out, seized the pencil and turned it over so that the eraser end was resting in the bottom of the pocket and the sharpened end was upright. He quickly moved on and I was too surprised by the action to thank him. For the most part, respectable citizens, busy with their daily activities, simply ignored the foreign soldiers in their midst. As a result, many of our men considered the French to be snobbish. I felt this was denied by the fact that if an American soldier needed assistance, for example needed directions to a location, any citizen he accosted seemed eager to help. As for snobbishness, I only encountered it on one occasion and the snob was not French. A British officer, a lieutenant (I believe they pronounce that Lef-tenent) and his driver entered our motor pool in an American-made armored car and requested help for an electrical problem. I was sent to help them. As it turned out the only problem was that they did not understand the array of controls for lights, heater, wiper and such on the dashboard. When I set about explaining what they needed to know I addressed my first comments to the officer. This was apparently a social gaffe. He looked positively distraught and yelled at the driver, "Do you understand what the American Corporal is <u>telling you</u>? I quickly switched to speaking directly to the driver, presumably my peer, not to the exalted one, the officer. I think the driver may have been fuddled by my American accent, but I noted the lieutenant was now listening attentively.

Of course we observed French customs that differed considerably from our own. Earlier I mentioned the amusement with which we observed the elderly man in the small village peeing against a wall in plain view of other villagers both male and female. We had by now leaned that this was not indicative of senile mental decline—it was a relatively common practice for men of all age groups. In French houses where we had been billeted, the indoor toilet usually consisted of a hole in the floor. One of our philosopher types pointed out that squatting over such a hole several times a day must be good exercise for legs---keeping them shapely, in the case of young women and keeping them supple into old age. In the central squares of larger towns we encountered the *pissoire*. This distinctive looking small structure was for men only, encouraging them to step out of sight while taking care of their urinary needs. Then one day a young woman approached a small group of our men on the street and asked if one of us would give her a condom. This request could easily have been mistaken for a novel come-on by an enterprising prostitute but as it turned out the woman had an injured finger which had been freshly bandaged with white cloth. She wanted to put a condom over the bandage to keep it clean. One of my comrades searched his pockets, came up with the requested item, and the young woman thanked him and went away.

There was no doubt the French had a more relaxed attitude toward bodily functions than Americans did. Just how relaxed may be demonstrated by a story told by one of our medical technicians who had an experience that was totally embarrassing for him but seemed to be completely acceptable to a French couple of his acquaintance. He had been called several times to serve as an interpreter for our officers in their dealings with the mayor of a small town where we were staying. During this duty he met both the mayor and the mayor's wife, who was apparently helping out with the work of the mayor's office. One day after his duty was finished he started to walk back to the area where we were billeted. As he walked through the battered town he realized that he was in urgent need of a toilet and as his path at that time led across a block where large buildings had been demolished by bombs, he sought privacy between two mounds of bricks. But then he realized someone else was coming toward him along the path and would pass only a few yards from where he was now crouching with his drawers and trousers down around his ankles. It was too late for him to spring up and rearrange his clothing so he decided to remain as he was and hope the approaching stranger or strangers would do the polite thing and pretend not to see him. But then, to his horror, he saw that the two people approaching him were not strangers—they were the mayor of the town and his wife with whom he had been exchanging pleasantries only an hour or so earlier. But there was noting he could do except crouch absolutely still and wait for them to pass. The peak of his embarrassment had not yet arrived, for as the couple came to their closest point the mayor beamed at him and called out a friendly greeting and—horror of horrors!—the wife, walking on the other side of her husband, leaned forward as if for a better view and greeted him, her face lit by a friendly smile. As they passed, he found himself muttering, "Bon jour, Bon jour," in a subdued, unnatural-sounding voice. When he told this story to comrades that evening he finished with, "Thank God, they didn't decide to stop and chat for a while!"

CHAPTER 19

AN INTERLUDE IN LORRAINE

When I came downstairs the usual after-dinner bull session was underway and tonight the subject being debated was love. Buba and Mark were both trying to talk at once, and Harry was sitting quietly, with an expression of tolerant amusement like a parent listening to young children argue about something they don't understand. Mark, a chronic teller of lurid tales about his sexual conquests, was arguing that there is no such thing as love. Curiously, Buba, known to be a womanizer of extraordinary persistence and probable success, seemed to be quite angry about this. He turned to me and said, "Tell this heah damn Yankee he crazy as hell---he say theah ain't no such thing as love."

"Hey, leave me out of this," I said, "You guys are the experts, but if you can't agree, ask Harry. He's read a lot of books on the subject, may even have done research."

Buba said, "How 'bout it, Harry. Ain't I right?"

There was a pause, after which Harry said, "Well. you see, the problem here is one of definition. To some people love is just a physiological state---like that of a tomcat yowling on the back fence, a state of urgent desire, a need for just any female cat right now, tonight.

On a higher level, the love expounded by poets and song writers, by countless movie plots, involving long term caring, tenderness, wanting to give exclusive devotion to just one person, well, you have to experience it to believe it. Yes, you see, love does exist, though I can understand how men intent on trying to connect with everything that wears a skirt may have reason to doubt it."

Buba yelled, "See theah! Ah'm right!"

Mark yelled, "Watttayuhmean, yer right? Yer th' one that zero's in on every broad in sight. I wouldn't trust you alone with my grandmother!"

I felt a sudden longing for the quiet out-of- doors. I slipped out, unnoticed, into the tiny, bare front yard of the miner's row-house. Soon the sun would be down and in the cave-like darkness of a blacked-out city there would be nothing to see. Reggie was at the curb working on the recon-captain's jeep. The vehicle had an unusual name painted under the windshield—"Happy Bottom". I knew the story back of that. The driver, a personable young fellow from one of the Ivy League schools, had asked the captain's permission to put his girlfriend's name on the jeep. The captain had said, "Good idea. Only we'll put my wife's name on it. Take it over to the motor pool now and get it done. Her name is Gladys. Be sure they spell it right, G-L-A-D-Y-S."

The driver went off to the motor pool brooding angrily about the injustice of having to have "his" jeep christened "Gladys" instead of "Kimberly." It was especially galling since he had made the suggestion and his idea had been stolen from him. . When the jeep came back from the painter it bore the inscription: HAPPY BOTTOM. The driver was braced to take his punishment but the captain just looked at the name and laughed. Maybe it was a pet name for his wife.

Now Reggie had the hood up and was bending over the engine compartment, reaching far down inside. He straightened up and gave me an angry look. "Hey," he said, "How come I'm stuck with working overtime on this damned jeep and you're already dressed up for a night on the town?"

"I guess its fate," I said. "Some of us were born under a lucky star— others under a truck. Look at it this way, the captain always thinks of you when there's an important job to be done, right? Well, when the time comes to break the master sergeant down to buck private—which will be any day now—who will the captain think of to take his place?"

"That'll be the day", Reggi muttered. "Make me master sergeant and there won't be anybody to do the dirty work."

I was turning to wander off when movement at an upstairs window across the narrow street caught my attention. A girl's face had appeared. For just an instant my eyes met her's, then she stepped back from the window, disappearing behind the frame on one side. In a walk through the streets of the town , the previous evening, I had seen girls standing in windows who wanted to be seen, and I had felt revulsion—and pity. But this girl had withdrawn instantly when she realized she was looking into the eyes of a foreign soldier. The vision of her face was fixed in my mind as if I had snapped a photograph with my eyes: a pale oval framed by dark hair, large, surprised eyes, a shapely mouth. And now she peeked around the side of the window and, seeing that I was still looking, slipped quickly out of sight again. The window was open—there was no glass to interfere with the sound of my voice— so I called up to her, "Mademoiselle, voulez-vous prendre une promenade dans la ville?"

I knew that all civilians were under a strict curfew and could only leave their homes after six P. M. unless accompanied by a soldier. The girl came back into full view, looked down at me, and spoke in English, very seriously, without smiling, "One moment—I come—down."

She promptly appeared on the front stoop, accompanied by another girl and a woman old enough to be their mother. The other girl had the unkempt look of the women coal miners and the mother had a curiously bloated face, but the girl from the window was a cameo of youth and health; shapely, pretty, sweet-looking, with a shy air that contradicted the promptness with which she had responded to my invitation to take a walk. She was wearing a simple dress, the hemline above her knees. We soldiers had observed appreciatively the short skirts of French girls that season. It was, I suspected, not so much a matter of local style or custom as a reflection of the fact that girls in their upper teens or early twenties had grown taller while waiting for an opportunity to buy new clothes. Her dark hair was arranged in the soft-looking waves affected by movie actresses of the years just before the war. Her whole appearance was strangely out of place here —it was as though a pretty American girl had magically appeared on this grubby street.

Every face in the trio was smiling warmly, as if welcoming the first liberating Yank they had had an opportunity to thank. Mamma and Sister were speaking in that pleasant-sounding, Alsatian French which their Nazi overlords had forbidden them to speak in public. Lydia was demonstrating her school-girl English—speaking slowly, precisely, as if reciting for a strict teacher. Mamma spoke to me in French and Lydia translated: "You must come back soon. It will be dark soon."

The three women suddenly darted back through the door, chattering excitedly, then Papa appeared. He was a thin, gaunt coal miner. Every pore in his face was a distinct black dot and his hair was stiff like short brush bristles. He was regarding me in a friendly manner and said something in German of which I understood only the final "sehr gut." I interpreted this as a father's blessing on the planned walk.

Lydia came out alone, now wearing a sweater against the night's chill, and we strolled away, ignoring the envious stare of Reggie. We turned a corner and walked through a block where buildings lay in ruins and the air smelled of burned wood. What a strangely misplaced couple we would have seemed if there had been someone to see us in that bleak environment. She like a pretty college girl just arrived from New York or Paris. I in my new Eisenhower jacket with red engineer braid on my cap and my trousers tucked into new, illegal paratrooper boots. (These had been issued to us but we had been warned to keep them covered by our trousers if real paratroopers were around!) The broken sidewalk was a good excuse for her to take a firm grip on my arm. As we went along together we talked animatedly in a mixture of her high school English and my college French. She talked about her family. The other girl, whom I had thought was older than she, was actually a younger sister who had been working in the mines for a few years. She, Lydia, was excused from such work because she had been a good student in high school. Her mother and father wanted her to have a clean job in an office and never have to work in the mines. By being a good student she had found for herself, here in this drab and colorless environment, hope for a better life.

Earlier that day, riding in from the west in our trucks, we had remarked on the squalor of this miners' suburb in the western, French, fringe of the border city of Saarbrucken. Some blocks had been devastated by bombs, but even where damage was minimum the buildings were ancient and grimed with coal dust. The people on the streets had a grim and scruffy look. I had seen two small boys in ragged clothing fighting in the street, gripping rocks in their hands as weapons. One urchin, nine years old perhaps, received a blow to the head and staggered away from the fight, wild eyed with pain. The other boys laughed at his distress. Hungry children had turned up to beg at the army chow line. Our men were generous, giving away their bread, or anything that could be lifted from the plate and handed to a child. Then, that afternoon, Headquarters Company had gone to the mine exit to bathe. The miners association had invited us to use their shower room. And it would be appreciated, the captain said, if we would leave some soap behind. The miners had had no soap for a long time. No wonder Lydia's sister, at the age of seventeen, looked much older.

The street was darkening now, softening the edges of the ruins, hiding the blackened facades of the standing buildings. A cool breeze brought the odor of countryside outside the town. Lydia wanted to know about my family in far-away America. She wanted to know if we had a car. That was one of those wonder-things she had heard about people in America. All of them had cars! I described our family cars, three in all. *I* didn't mean to brag---it was just facts---and a thing of wonder to her.

We came to the street of shops and went into the canteen that had been established in an undamaged restaurant. We sat in a booth and drank real American Coca-Cola.   I had not spoken to a girl for three months---not since England. Now Lydia was sitting here, across from me, her big brown eyes fixed on my face, trying to understand everything I said. Her voice was a delight to hear---the drum-beat rhythm of French---every syllable stressed the same, or her schoolgirl English with many words accented in the wrong place

I realized I was staring at her, entranced, while she was speaking. She kept dropping her glance downward and to the side, shyly, as she talked. I got up and moved around the little table and sat beside her. There was a pleasant perfume about her—I wondered if precious cologne had been hoarded for years for a special occasion. Her nails were neatly trimmed —her hair was clean and shining. Somehow the humble miners' daughter was managing to uphold the French middle class woman's tradition for good grooming. I could feel her warmth against my side and soon I was holding her small, soft hand. Walking home through the blacked-out streets she hugged my arm firmly. On the stoop before her front door, when I leaned down to kiss her, she lifted her face willingly. As I crossed the street to my own quarters I remembered how I had felt after that first kiss on a high-school date.

CHAPTER 20

POLITICS AND LIQUOR

The young Frenchman leaned forward in his chair and directed his question to Harry. I was surprised that I understood exactly what he said. To my untrained ears, most sentences delivered by native speakers were an explosion of vaguely familiar words from which I struggled to extract the meaning. The question was, "Que pensez- vous aux grands industriels?" (What do you think of the great industrialists?)

For Harry, the question was like the pop of the starter's pistol at a track meet. He was off and running on one of his favorite topics—the exploitation of workers by rich capitalists. I found his French, delivered with an American accent, at about one half the speed of a native speaker, was easily understandable.

"All their wealth should be confiscated. They should be assigned to menial labor. If they refuse to work they should be shot. All means of production should belong to the workers who produce."

I was a little shocked at the ferocity of his answer. Harry was known to be a gentle person. I could not imagine him expressing anger at one of his comrades. He was a generous contributor of chewing gum and candy to the child beggars who often surrounded us. He detested having to carry a weapon. I decided he was only trying to impress the young miner who quite probably was, as many French workers were, a member of the communist party. Harry once told me he had been a member of a young communist group when in High school. He hinted darkly that the army had a dossier on his activities and he would never be promoted above the rank of corporal. It was my opinion that he had not been promoted because the master-sergeant didn't like him. This may have been ethnic bias---Harry was Jewish --or simply because he spoke like an educated person. His proper use of the subjunctive mood may well have angered our educationally-challenged master sergeant from the hills of west Texas.

I had little interest in this discussion, having heard Harry's views on the subject many times and I had somewhere else to go. Across the street, in another company house, Lydia was expecting me. There the discussion would be of much greater practical value—improvement in my French, a polishing of pronunciation in her already good English.

Later that night, I returned to find Harry alone in the downstairs parlor sitting at a table with an opened book and an almost empty bottle of liquor in front of him. He was sipping from a glass and his face had an unnatural, dark redness. He looked at me through squinted eyes as if he were irritated by the dim light from the room's single bare light bulb. He said, "Well, did you make out this time?"

I said, "She's a nice girl Harry, Furthermore, her mother never leaves the room when I'm there."

"A nice French girl. Ha! And a coal miners daughter! Surely a bourgeoisie man who dallies with a girl of the proletariat does not have honorable intentions."

"I resent that, Harry. Leedee may be from a humble background but she has lifted herself by her own efforts. She was an A student in high school—a French high school you should note with respect. She has acquired a usefull level of fluency in two foreign languages, and has mastered the typewriter and the adding machine. There will be no coal dust in her ears, no black lungs in her future."

Harry looked thoughtful for a moment. He said, "She's pretty now, but have you taken a good look at her mother? That puffy face denotes some kind of glandular trouble. Likely to be hereditary."

"So? I'm not planning to stay here and breed recruits for the French Army. We're good friends. She tutors me in French and practices her

English—which she already speaks with more attention to grammatical correctness than most of our learned colleagues in headquarters company. What is that stuff you're drinking, Harry?"

He said, "It's harmless—tastes like some kind of fruit syrup— probably not intoxicating. Alfonse brought it over as a gift. We were having a comradely drink but he had to leave early—has to get up early for work in the mine." His voice took on a hasher tone as he continued: "Has to labor sixteen hours a day so fat exploiters of the working class can have their mansions, limousines, and artificial-blonde wives and mistresses."

I knew Harry was not a drinker. I had never known him to take an interest even in beer. I examined the bottle. "My god, Harry this is schnapps. One glass of this stuff could put you in a coma."

He said, "Leaders of the party must to be able to hold their liquor. Party bigwigs toast each other all evening. I propose a toast now—to the revolution—he emptied the glass."

I was at a loss for words. Should I go upstairs and recruit some of our room mates to help me drag him up to bed? I tugged his arm, tentatively. He shook me off.

Now he seemed really angry. He glared at me and said in a tense unnatural voice. "Do you know why I talk to you about politics so much?"

I said," Sure, it's because I'm a good listener. When you use one of those six syllable words that no one in this outfit has ever heard, I nod my head and pretend to agree."

"No," he said, "It's because if I could convert you, I could convert anyone."

"Gee, Harry, is that a compliment or an insult?"

" It's not a compliment. You see, you are indubitably the prototypical, politically naive, non-cerebral, sports-loving American college student— the kind who is likely to confuse Karl Marx with one of the Marx brothers. "

Well! I was trying to make allowances for his condition, but this did miff me. I wondered if the liquor was acting like truth serum, removing his inhibitions and letting him say what he really thought of me.

I said, somewhat testily, "I admire the Marx Brothers; they're smart cookies and make a lot of money. As for Karl, he was a scruffy, unwashed loser who should have been jailed early on with no access to paper and pen."

Harry bristled, "Now you've gone too far. You think I won't remember this when I sober up. Well, I won't forget it and you needn't consider me a friend any more."

With that, as if to convey his contempt for my opinions, even advice about drinking, he poured the rest of the liquor into the glass and gulped it down. I decided it was time to leave him to his fate. He could sleep off his drunkenness in a chair or on the floor as well as in his sleeping bag upstairs. As I walked to the stairs he yelled after me, "And give back all my books that you have!"

This last statement indicated he had lost touch with reality. I had only one of his books. It was a copy of Julian Huxley's *Evolution, The Modern Synthesis.* Harry had bought it in an English bookstore, probably because he knew Karl Marx had been an admirer of Darwin, but had become bored with the accounts of changes in pigeons, rabbits, finches and other creatures dear to the heart of a biologist. He had given the book to me. I still have it.

Next morning I found Harry in his usual work place beside the noisy generator that furnished power for the welder. As usual, he had an open book in his hands. I supposed he was memorizing the declension of a German verb.

He looked up as I approached and said, "Boy, I have a terrible headache. I think I must be coming down with something."

I said, "It could be meningitis; it starts that way. You better go see the medics and get a sulfa pill as soon as possible." (We had been given sulfanilamide pills in England when there was fear of an outbreak of meningitis.)

He said, " I'll be through with this job in about fifteen minutes and I'll go over and see the doctor."

I saw him later in the day, He said, "Well, I did see a doctor. He gave me a couple of aspirins and said I would be alright tomorrow."

"Well, I guess you'll be alright then"

He answered, "Yeah, we'll be alright."

We were.

CHAPTER 21

FAREWELL TO LORRAINE

I saw Lydia every night. Curiously, the other men of the motor pool, living there in the house across the street, made no move to flirt with her. There was a sort of gentlemen's agreement that she was my girl. But of course, from their stories, they had social projects of their own underway elsewhere in the neighborhood. I was learning about the quaint courtship customs of the locals. I found it was permissible to hug Lee-dee and nuzzle up for an occasional kiss while seated on the family sofa with her mother across the room pretending not to notice us. It was an idea I had to get used to. The first time we were alone, snuggling on the sofa, and Maman walked in, I drew away with embarrassment. Lydia let me know, with a peeved expression and a tightening of her hugging arm, that I was not supposed to draw away. I was a quick learner for this sort of thing. Soon we would sit on the sofa, in a world of our own, talking softly, my arm around her, exchanging an occasional kiss, while the business of the house went on around us. Even Papa coming in from work did not interrupt the tête-à-tête for long. He always gave me a serious, friendly look and usually remembered to say "Bon Jour" instead of "Guten Abend". But he went into another room while I was there, as though chaperoning was not his responsibility. As for *Maman,* she ignored us but she was always nearby. Whether such chaperoning was standard for this social group or something they had worked out for Lydia and her foreign soldier, I never knew. Some of my companions told raunchy stories of being invited to use the bedroom,

93

but I suspected this was just more of the fictitious braggadocio which often decorated their conversations.

One day I came in and found Lydia was being besieged by a local suitor, a thin young fellow with a miner's complexion and hair. Lydia was washing dishes and seemingly trying to ignore the local swain who was speaking German loudly in the manner of a person who likes the sound of his own voice. His idea of the romantic approach was to slap her hard on a hip, then laugh loudly at her protest.

I was astonished by the first slap, enraged by the second, and was considering giving him the bum's rush out the kitchen door—although I knew that wouldn't look good because he was so small. Fortunately, *Maman* came in, sized up the situation at a glance and said something to the local gallant in harsh sounding German that sent him on his way.

Perhaps *Maman* didn't want to lose me. I had brought her soap from company supply, and coffee and sugar from the mess hall—the mess sergeant was sympathetic to all lovers—and who knows what her hopes were for Lydia. A mother has to give up her daughter sooner or later. What better way than to send her to far-off, wonderful America.

But, of course, this was the army, and soon I had to move on. It seemed remarkable that we had stayed there in one place for almost two weeks. The Colonel had been heard to complain that ours was the forgotten battalion. Tanks and infantry were being rushed to the expanding front deep inside Germany but there was no need now for our specialty as combat engineers: blowing up roads and felling trees and walls in the path of enemy tanks. The motorized legions of Nazi blitzkrieg would never charge again.

There may have been another reason for our lack of movement. We were out of gas. Gasoline that was to be delivered to our seventh army forces was being diverted, it was said, to Patton's third army, to the tanks that were furiously blasting their way across Germany. It may well have been that our supply people had not anticipated the speed with which our armies would advance once they were inside Germany. Certainly the Nazi's had been expected to make a really determined stand inside their own homeland. This did not happen. The much discussed redoubt in the natural mountain fortress of the Bavarian Alps, the expected last stand of a desperate nation, did not occur. Our seventh army and the French Army on our right flank had changed the direction of advance from east to southeast in anticipation of increasing resistance in the alpine foothills. Instead, the Nazi forces facing our advance simply melted away in the closing weeks of the war with only small spots of resistance here and there.

But the day finally came when our battalion had to move on. I walked with Lydia for the last time on a sunny morning when the first pale green leaves were appearing on the damaged trees. We stood on her door stoop to say farewell. She pressed a tiny gift into my hand. It was a lapel pin in the form of a cross—a cross with two horizontal bars—the Cross of Lorraine. She said, "Now Lorraine will always be free." Those words seemed to make it a gift, not to me personally, but to the army I represented—the Army that had freed her country. We had never believed that our association was anything more than a fleeting interlude that would surely end very soon. Every time we said goodnight, there was a possibility that I would be gone the next day. There was a sense of unreality about the whole affaire— as though she were only a soldier's dream that had to end with the wake up call. I must have missed her desperately in the days that followed our separation, yet I cannot recall this. Yes, stangely, I cannot recall that I missed her! One day she was in my arms, there on her doorstep in the warm sunlight, murmuring "Aujourd'hui ist le premier jour de printemps." (Today is the first day of spring.) The next day it was as though she had never existed.

Months later, when I was back in America, I received the only letter from her. She wanted me to know she had a job in a lawyer's office and was happy because now she could help her family. The job was in St Avold, and she was riding her bicycle to work, a round trip of sixteen kilometers every day. She included a tiny poem of only four short lines. It rimed in the original French, but not, of course, in the English translation.

> Near to a clear spring,
> a timid flower blooms.
> And it says, very softly,
> Do not forget me.

CHAPER 22

THE STORY TELLER

Buba was a rustic raconteur. Ask him a question and he would launch into a story replete with hints about a bucolic life style quiet foreign to most of his listeners. One evening he told us how it came to pass that he had volunteered for military service instead of waiting, as most of us had, to be drafted. The story went like this: The winter of forty one-forty two in the Carolina Mountains was a bad one. Not only were people snow bound for weeks, when spring came the flooding creeks and washed out roads kept his whole family locked in their isolated cove for added weeks with no chance to escape. One evening after supper his Paw, reminiscing about the days of his youth, came up with a bit of information that grabbed Buba's attention. "You know," he said, "that left hand mule was broke to saddle when he was a colt. In fact I used to ride him to town."

At this point, one of his army buddies interrupted Buba too ask how you know if a mule is left handed. He diverted from his story to explain that when you harness a team to the plow you always put the same mule on the left and the other one on the right. He declared, "They get bothered if you switch 'em and they don't pull worth shucks."

He continued his story, saying, after hearing his paw's remark he could hardly wait for morning. Up early, he went out to the barn and threw a saddle on the designated mule. Though years had passed since the critter had felt this burden on it back, it merely turned its head, looked at Buba with mild interest, and then continued munching its oats. When he tightened the girth, the mule puffed itself up with air, a common ploy of experienced mounts protecting themselves from too tight a squeeze around their middles. But in this case, it was a trick the mule had learned years before, and had not forgotten! So it was no surprise to Buba that when he sprang up into the saddle and clucked at the mule to go—it went! He rode off hollering, "I'm free at last!"

The road was too muddy for any vehicle, even his dad's trusty old ford truck, and had dangerous stretches where a horse might lose its footing and slide down a slope into a flooding creek. But the mule, he claimed, was so sure footed it could walk a tight rope if it had to. Arriving at the center of the town—which he did not name—he tethered his mule to a hitching post in front of the courthouse and was immediately hailed by the county sheriff who was chatting with friends on the courthouse steps. The sheriff approached him and the conversation went like this:

"You the Owens kid from Coon Holler, right?"

"That's me."

"I'll bet yer mor'en eighteen years old."

"Ah am, ah am."

"Let me see your draft card, Son."

"Whut's that?"

"Don't you know they's a wah on, Boy?"

"A wah? You mean them damn Yankees is invadin us again?"

"Nah, its the Germans."

"The Germans! My paw went off to fight them before I was born. He said they were licked for good!"

"Not good enough, I reckon. You come with me. They's a man across the street wants to see you."

The man across the street was sitting at a desk in the front of Peabody's Barber Shop. He was wearing an army uniform with a lot of stripes on his sleeves. He wrote down Buba's name and address, and congratulated him on volunteering for the U S army. He was quite friendly, informing Buba that as a volunteer he would get a zero in front of his number so everyone would know he had joined up because he wanted to serve his country instead of waiting to be drafted. "And the train will be here in about twenty minutes so get on down to the station."

Buba, who was fond of animals, finished his story by wondering what became of the mule. He blamed himself for not having remembered to untie it so it could find its way home.

After he joined out outfit, Buba was assigned to drive a huge tank recovery vehicle which we called the wreaker. We believed the assignment came to him because of his large size. He was over six feet tall and had broad shoulders and rugged features. People asked him if he had played football in high school. He was evasive about answering this, leading us to believe he never gone to high school. In an engineer headquarters company where most men had had at least two years of college and, or had been in an Armed Services Training Program (ASTP) on a university campus for a few months, he seemed somewhat out of place, but this did not bother him. Sergeant Harris, the motor pool supply clerk, who sometimes used Buba as a driver when picking up supplies, declared he was an excellent driver. Harris declared this was because Buba had no thoughts in his head to distract him. But we knew Harris was biased against people like Buba. He was from Nashville and felt impelled to tell everyone that he had never listened to the Grand Old Oprey on the radio, much less attended it. And it was not true that Buba had no thoughts—those of us who had to listen to his bragging in nightly bull sessions knew that he thought about women most of the time. We thought many of the stories he told of his amorous adventures were made up or borrowed from the tales told by other womanizers.

Somewhere in France he acquired a tiny dog. It was a miniature Chihuahua, if there is such a breed, the smallest dog I had ever seen. When he drove the big wrecker he carried the dog inside his shirt, its tiny face looking out the opening provided by leaving one button unbuttoned. Sometimes he had to leave the dog for a while and when he came back to it, it danced around him crazily in a seeming paroxysm of joy, making squeaking noises as if trying to talk. We suspected he had acquired the dog to use in attracting the attention of women. Whatever the initial intent, he and the dog soon bonded to one another; they became inseparable.

CHAPTER 23

LOST IN THE BLACK FOREST

Sad Sack was our secret name for the new motor officer. He joined our outfit while we were in France and had immediately settled in as a non-functioning member of the motor pool. He served no useful purpose that we could see. His days were spent chain smoking and reading novels. He infuriated the machinist by appropriating the work bench in the machine shop truck for his bed. Each morning he left his rumpled sleeping bag on the bench for the machinist to roll up and put away. The machine shop had to be ready for inspection at any time and the machinist couldn't risk having another officer, even Mr. Spode, drop in for a surprise inspection and find an unmade bed decorating a critical work area. Sad Sack sometimes muttered commands to whatever enlisted man was nearest, usually a request for some item or service to add to his own comfort. He didn't bother to learn anyone's name but simply pointed a finger and said "You" to select the unwary enlisted man who had wandered too close.

The master sergeant, sensitive for once to something that was angering the men, attempted to explain why Sad Sack was dawdling away the hours in our midst. He declared that the table of organization for an engineer headquarters company called for a commissioned officer, a captain, to head up the motor pool. Though Sad Sack was only a second lieutenant (and we thought it unlikely that he would ever be promoted) he was presumably filling the shoes of that motor officer. Mr. Spode was now second in command, though he had acted like the supreme authority in the motor pool for all the months since the activation of the battalion. Now he, the experienced leader, had to accept the fact that he had become number two, subject to the commands of the inert and apparently incompetent lieutenant.

We, the men of the motor pool, now assembled for a speech by the master sergeant, listened glumly as he explained, "Them officers is jest here so they ken take over in case somethin happens to me. I'm the boss you have to watch out for 'cause I know whut needs to be done in this man's motor pool and I aim to get it done. Sometimes Spode—uh, Mr. Spode, passes me information from headquarters like whur we're gonna go next and when to leave—stuff like that. But nobody messes with how I run the motor pool."

A few days later we had a chance to witness this chain of command in action. It was Easter Sunday, 1945, a fine spring day, no doubt a fine day for religious celebration, but for the army a fine day for travel. When we finished breakfast the trucks were lined up in the village street in convoy formation. There was a scramble to get aboard and I found myself sharing the space in the back of the lead vehicle with four other men, including the loquacious and seemingly omnipresent Joe B. The trucks were loaded up, ready to roll out to our next destination when Sad Sack and Spode came wheeling up in a staff car. They were seated in the back seat of the vehicle with a small, grim looking driver at the wheel. The master sergeant hastened to the side of the car and stood there at exaggerated attention. Spode handed him a map and delivered a few terse commands, after which the two officers and their driver went roaring off down the highway to the east, presumably on their way to our next destination.

They were leaving the master sergeant in charge of four or five trucks forming the rearguard, not in any combat sense, but to give assistance to any battalion vehicles that broke down en route. We watched him spread the map on the flat hood of the lead vehicle and then caress it repeatedly with the end of his index finger. That handy pointer seemed to be following a different route across the map each time with many hesitations along the way. Two concerned onlookers, T4's who had not yet boarded the lead truck, moved up to stand beside him and peer over his elbows. Raising his head to glare, first at one, then at the other, he said, "Yew boys think I need yur help readin' this map?"

Both men seemed abashed, they turned their gaze to other features of the landscape, each waiting for the other to answer the question. We all knew the master sergeant was sensitive about the fact that many of the enlisted men in headquarters company were, to use his own contemptuous term, " college boys," who had wasted their time as over-aged school boys while he had attended the school of hard knocks, first as a cowboy, then to a C C C camp and then to the army. He never ceased trying to prove he was smarter than the men under him.

Soon he folded—more correctly, wadded—the map and stuffed it into the pocket of his field jacket. He then assumed the characteristic stance which meant he was going to give an order. This involved standing at attention, while holding his hands out from his sides as if his arms were too muscle bound to hang down properly. We called this his gunfighter's stance. He thrust out his thick chin, in the way that always reminded me of the pictures of Mussolini, and glared down the line of trucks suspiciously, as if seeking some driver who was not paying attention. Next he bawled, in a high-pitched, nasal tone, "Wind em' up, Boys!" I suppose there was an official command for this action but, if so, we never heard it. Starters snarled, engines roared, and the few men who had not yet boarded, scrambled into their places.

We were off, rolling eastward, deeper into Hitler's collapsing realm. It was a peculiarity of the Dodge three-quarter-ton truck that there was no barrier between the front seat—the cab on most trucks—and the men seated in the bed of the truck. The master sergeant was in the front seat with his own chosen driver—a bone-thin hillbilly whose surly lips leaked tobacco juice. I heard the sergeant say, "We gonna go right over them hills over there."

"Them hills" I knew from studying my own small map—the sort of map you might find in a school geography book, showing railroads as red lines but no highways—were the northern ridges of the Schwartzwald, the legendary Black Forest, where men smoked big, curvy pipes and carved wooden cuckoo clocks. I was looking forward to a day of interesting scenery. With every mile we had gone eastward from the crowded Rhineland the landscape had become more attractive. It was, I thought, as if some master artist had created a painting of an idealized land with forests, fields and villages all blending harmoniously into a masterpiece. I reflected on the difference in America. In Arkansas for example where we had had our engineer training---human habitations, all too often, form ugly scars on an otherwise pleasant landscape. Here in this ancient farmland even the barns were decorative. I found myself staring at one that had a huge mural painted on one side. It was a scene of mountains, trees and meadows. Everyone in the truck was quiet, staring at the scenery. Even Joe, for once, had nothing to say. I was in a sort of waking dream as I gazed at the unfolding panorama.

Soon after we entered the forested mountains, we came into a village where the people fled for cover as soon as they saw us. Three small children, standing outside the front door of a house, were dressed in elaborate Easter costumes. No adults were to be seen but the children stood there motionless, like small statues, their eyes fixed on our approaching trucks. A woman dashed out the door, scooped up the smallest child, shrieked commands at the other two and rushed her little brood indoors.

One of my companions called out, tensely, "Damit, Sergeant, these people have never seen G I trucks before!" The Master Sergeant dug the now-crumpled map out of his pocket and began to re-study it. The driver pulled his "Monkey Ward Gun"—our name for the small machine gun with a folding metal stock carried by some drivers—from its rack above the windshield and laid it across his knees. There was a sudden scramble in the back of the truck as five "college boy" technicians, who had never fired a shot in anger, clawed at their gear, and snapped ammunition clips into their carbines.

I found I had developed an even more intense interest in the landscape, particularly the patches of dark forest that were interspersed with the neat fields. Or would an attack come from back of a cluster of farm buildings—or even from the windows of village houses as we were passing? The steeple of a church was suddenly transformed from picturesque to threatening. That bell tower would be just right for a sniper ready to fire at men in trucks on the highway below.

The Master Sergeant growled, "We ain't lost, I see whur we are— they's another crossroad jist ahead—if we hang a left we can swing back toward the main road out of Ross-tat. (The sergeants' attempts to pronounce the names of German towns were usually good for a secret laugh, but not now.)

I think the same thought must have occurred to all of us who heard him: we should have been on that main road all the time. Joe called out, with a peculiar shrillness in his voice, "Lets just turn around and go back the way we came!" The sergeant turned around in his seat and glared at him. "S'matter, Bosco? Got shit in yer blood?" Evidently, the stubborn sergeant would rather risk the lives of everyone than lose face by turning back.

We did come to a crossroad, and we turned left, but it was a narrower, more winding road than the one we had been following. And it seemed to go on and on interminably between towering walls of German pines. It looped around mountainous curves to reveal more gloomy woods where whole divisions of murderous SS troops could be lurking. We passed through other villages and saw frightened faces peeking at us past the edges of drawn curtains.

There was plenty of time for somber thoughts, like the irony of being killed on Easter Sunday, a beautiful spring day, with the war almost over. How unfair that this group of soldiers, any one of whom could have read the map and followed the correct course, was being driven to its doom by an illiterate redneck who probably couldn't have found his way from Fort Worth to Dallas without stopping several times to ask for directions.

At last, after driving down a particularly long, gloomy valley between walls of forest, we came to another crossroad where a wider pavement led off to the east. To our great joy we saw that the road shoulders were strewn with familiar American litter. The vast multitudes of the 21st Corps, swarming to the east, had ridden here discarding their empty food cartons, cigarette wrappers, tin cans and other waste from their vehicles onto the neatly-mowed grass beside the road.

It was Joe who expressed our relief from tension, he yelled "Look at that mess! We're home again!"

In the midst of nervous laughter, someone shouted, "Speak for yourself, Joe! You're the only one here from from New Jersey!"

Beside the next turnoff we spotted the small marker placed by our recon section and soon our lead truck pulled up beside the familiar guidon of our engineer battalion. The little red flag was waving on its standard in front of a village school.

The sergeant , thoughtlessly—or perhaps because he didn't want to be queried by an officer about why we were so late—sent Joe in to inquire where the motor pool was to be located.

Joe was gone quite a while. He came back, looking happy, accompanied by our colorful executive officer, Colonel B.—secretly called Rhett Butler by the men, and known for his habit of carrying a swagger stick. Knowing Joe, I was sure he had blurted out a dramatic story of how we had probed behind enemy lines led by our fearless Master Sergeant who had misread the map. Colonel B. confirmed this by impaling our leader with a steely look and saying, "Well, Sergeant, it looks like we are going to have to get you a seeing-eye dog! Next time let your driver read the map—or turn it over to Corporal Bosco." He flashed our group a broad, politicians smile. We knew he had been the mayor of a small town somewhere in the south. He sometimes forgot himself when speaking to a group of enlisted men and beamed genially, as if we were potential voters.

He said, "You're lucky to have made it, men. The French were supposed to secure the Black Forest two days ago, but they aren't keeping up with the schedule. Maybe they don't want to leave the Rhineland wine." We grinned politely.

We drove on to our assigned area. It was a gloomy-looking barracks building at the edge of the village. The German soldiers had fled without bothering to make up their beds. The latrine at the end of the building was in a filthy condition; the water supply had apparently failed quite some time before the Germans quit using the flush toilets.

The Master Sergeant went in to inspect and immediately yelled ," Corporal Bosko! Come here." His formal use of rank and last name was ominous. "Corporal, you're gonna clean this up. I want this latrine spic and span by eighteen hundred hours." He turned and walked out.

Joe stood there looking around, aghast. His face was red and furious, then he paled, probably a first symptom of impending illness. Before he set to work, I noticed he was looking at the dial of his watch and counting on his fingers, presumably converting the eighteen hundred hours to a non military number.

CHAPTER 24

WHO WOULD WANT TO SHOOT MR. SPODE?

Somewhere along the way Mr. Spode managed to acquire some large sheets of steel. These were of a thickness suggesting they might be able to stop a bullet or flying fragments from a explosion. He mobilized the resources of the motor pool to install these as armor plating around the bed of a three quarter ton Dodge. The result was a grotesquely deformed vehicle with a huge boxy shape back of the cab rising much higher than the standard bed cover of such a truck. It was also difficult to drive. Hit a rough patch on the highway and the whole top-heavy contraption would start swinging from side to side like a giant pendulum while the driver wrestled with the steering wheel to avoid assuming a zig zag course. No one wanted to drive it, but unfortunately it had to be used for regular supply missions. Concerns were expressed that its one of a kind appearance might inspire some combat hardened GI to fire a bazooka rocket at it. And why had this monstrosity been created? Why, to provide a more secure sleeping place for Mr. Spode!

One morning he summoned us to assemble for one of the morale lectures for which we saw little need. He informed us that we might be called upon to defend the motor pool against hostile German civilians. This, he said, might require firing on a mob including women and children.

We didn't believe him. As he walked away someone muttered, "I'll shoot that son of a bitch before I shoot a woman or kid." Later we had reason to believe he had heard the remark. The next time he called our squad together for a lecture he ended by giving us a strained smile and saying, "I understand at least one of you is planning to shoot me if we get into a combat situation." I suppose he was hoping for amused grins or chuckles at such an absurd idea. Every man in the group stood in silence looking solemnly at the ground or off into the distance. After a long pause, Spode turned and walked away.

We never, of course, encountered any threat of resistance by civilians. I noticed as we drove across the German countryside that our signal corps telephone wires were often lying exposed in ditches beside the road. Any German farmer with a patriotic grudge against us could have chopped those wires with a shovel or other farm implement. It didn't happen. Stop to ask a farmer for road directions, as I remember doing on at least two occasions, and he seemed eager to help. In fact the second of these launched into an account in faulty English about his relatives in America, an uncle in Pittsburg, I seem to remember. No German wanted us to think he had been involved in, or had even known about, the crimes of the Nazis. Only once did I witness an expression of anger toward our troops. In the city of Worms, among ruined buildings, I stood on a street corner and waited for a convoy of air corps trucks to pass. One of the trucks was pulling a large flat-bed trailer of the kind used for tank recovery. To my surprise, an officers' lounge had been set up on the flat surface of the trailer. It was fitted with sofas and chairs, a large table and a cabinet presumably holding the liquor. Young air corps officers were reclining at ease, smoking their cigarettes and observing the passing scene.

I heard angry exclamations from the German civilians who had stopped beside me to wait for the convoy to pass. One man shook his fist. I thought as the time that the anger was aroused by the sight of obviously looted furniture, but I later learned that while the typical German city dweller reacted to American ground troops with indifference, or even tried to be helpful, they had a smoldering rage against the flyers that had destroyed their cities and killed their relatives and neighbors. Twenty years later I was to hear an Austrian tour guide become emotional as he expressed his resentment against the American flyers who had dropped their bombs on innocent civilians. I refrained from reminding him that the German air force had been the first to launch murderous raids against innocent city dwellers, for example in the bombing of Rotterdam in 1940 and of many English cities early in the war. Actually the first very destructive bombing of a city was in 1937 when German planes, supporting the fascist forces of General Franco, bombed the Spanish city of Guernica.

CHAPTER 25

AN INCIDENT IN EDENKOBEN

Rumor had it that when we arrived in the German town of Edenkoben we were only two days behind the infantry. They had smoked out a sniper from the church tower, leaving the ancient structure pitted by bullets from their M1 rifles. Otherwise the town seemed undamaged by the wave of war that had washed over it.

Our engineer headquarters company moved into the town hall and other buildings around the central square. The Colonel occupied the burgomaster's office and sent a work detail up to the roof to remove a huge sign, a rampant eagle with a swastika clutched in its talons. When the sign was ready to fall, the men on the roof yelled "Fire in the hole!" the traditional warning that something is about to go Boom. The sign slid down the tile roof and crashed on the cobblestone pavement of the square. An elderly woman, dressed all in black, yelled shrilly from the sidewalk, "Es war dort zu lang bereits!" (It was there too long already.)

Apparently our little company of about one hundred forty men was the only American unit in the town, so the Colonel arranged for a show of force. He assigned everyone, drivers, clerks and technicians, to special guard duty. We were to walk in pairs up and down the main street, clad in our good O. D. (olive drab) uniforms with steel helmets on our heads and loaded carbines slung from our shoulders.

We were not accustomed to this kind of duty. The automotive mechanics, in particular, were bitter about having to clean themselves up and present a military appearance. One poor devil suddenly realized that he had not seen his carbine since leaving France several days earlier. He postponed the inevitable day of reckoning by borrowing a weapon from one of the cooks, the only ones excused from this warlike duty.

I was paired with Joe B. He was a reserve driver for the battalion officers but was idle most of the time since officers he had chauffeured never asked for him again. He was, as usual, chattering about unimportant things, apparently not even seeing the exotic sights around us. I was gaping at the quaint half-timbered buildings, studying the foreign signs on the shops, really intrigued by being surrounded by enemy civilians. There were elderly women dressed all in black, middle-aged business men in suits and hats, young women with well tended hair and short skirts, but no men or boys of military age. The people were walking in stony silence; there were no cheerful greetings, no casual conversation. There was only the sound of footsteps. A distant roar grew in volume and finally became recognizable as the sound of an approaching tank column. The monstrous machines, each marked with the white star of the American forces, came rolling right along the main street in an almost bumper to bumper procession. The civilians seemed to be ignoring the spectacle. Those walking along the street kept their eyes straight ahead, but some needed to cross the street and soon these were clustered in small groups on the street corners, like spectators of the passing show.

Joe found this amusing. He said, "I'll bet those Krauts are worried. They have to get home before curfew and they can't even get across the street. I'll bet we have miles of tanks coming up."

I looked at the expressionless faces and tried to imagine what they were thinking. What was it like, to stand in your own home town and watch this colossal display of the enemy's might? Being German, they may have been most impressed by the sheer untidiness of the passing scene. The tops of the tanks were cluttered with dirty duffel bags and carelessly rolled sleeping bags. Tank men in stained, rumpled fatigues were sprawling half out of the turrets, their eyes roving over the German crowd then fixing on any young woman in view. And how young they looked! Could it be that only the youngest soldiers could withstand the physical stress of bumping over the landscape inside those steel boxes? Even the thin-faced officer who was standing half out of a turret, his captains bars almost concealed by the crumpled collar of his field jacket, looked barely old enough to vote. Joe tried to make eye contact with him and saluted. The officer glared at him angrily.

Joe said, "Whatsamatter with that guy? He gave me a dirty look." I reminded him that officers in a combat zone don't appreciate being pointed out to snipers.

Joe looked worried. "Golly, do you think there are snipers here now---maybe in those upstairs windows over there?

I said, "Don't worry Joe. They're depending on you to spot targets for them."

Joe giggled nervously, and then launched into another long monologue. He had trouble making himself heard above the noise of the tanks so it was easy to ignore him. But suddenly he shouted right in my ear, "I have to find a latrine."

I said, "Tough luck, Joe, You're on guard duty 'till eighteen hundred hours." He stared at his wrist watch and counted on his fingers, presumably converting eighteen hundred hours to a civilian 6 P.M.

He yelled in my ear again, "We passed a restaurant back there and it was open. I'm gonna go back there and find the men's room."

I reminded him that our orders were to walk the street. Nothing had been said about entering buildings along the way. But he was insistent and I was remembering it was essential that partners stay together. I could be reprimanded for entering a restaurant, but if I lost sight of Joe and something happened to him I would be in real trouble.

So, I went with him into the foyer of the restaurant. There were the two doors labeled Herren and Damen. I shoved him toward the right one and followed him in. He disappeared into the single stall. There was a good mirror over the wash basin so I took off my helmet and set about combing my hair. This was no simple operation. Strong, yellow, G I soap had been a poor substitute for shampoo. The helmet-liner straps had set my hair in a pattern of stubborn cowlicks. While thus engaged I heard Joe muttering to himself inside the stall. I paid no attention until I heard him say, "I can't ever remember which way the safety catch is on--is it to the left, or to the right?"

The fool was sitting there tinkering with the safety on a loaded carbine. I said, "Joe, you push the safety catch with your trigger finger before you pull the trigger. So, to put it on safe, you have to push it the other way, right?" Apparently this explanation was too complicated for

Joe. The crack of the carbine was deafening in the confined space. The bullet drilled the wall about a foot from my head. Joe stumbled through the stall door yelling, "Oh my god! Did I hit you? Did I hit you?

I said, "No, you son of a bitch, but I'm going to hit you." But I wasn't really angry—there was the sort of euphoric feeling you get when lightening strikes nearby—your first thought is: It didn't hit me!

A middle aged man came rushing into the room—the owner, or manager, I supposed. He stood there looking at us questioningly. I felt some sort of explanation was in order. There was nothing in the phrase book to cover this situation but a sentence came into my mind from a deep well-spring of memory. My mother, as a child, had attended a bilingual school in central Missouri, a region settled in pioneer days by a multitude of German farmers. In later years she sometimes amused her own children with sayings she had learned from her little playmates. What I came up with was, "Meine kamerad ist ein dummkopf." I tapped my heard significantly—the universal gesture for loony. The German starred at Joe who was standing there, his eyes still wild with the horror of having almost murdered me. His trousers and drawers were down around his ankles exposing hairy legs and more. He was waving the carbine about distractedly. The man's expression changed. He seemed to be in the grip or a strong emotion—probably terror at being confronted by an armed madman. He turned and dashed out the door.

I urged Joe to get himself buttoned up and we moved out into the street trying to look nonchalant. The seemingly endless column of tanks was clanking thunderously over the pavement just beyond the narrow sidewalk. Another assortment of rough-riding kids was sprawled half out of the turrets scanning the crowd for girls. The German civilians were still waiting to cross the street. No one even glanced at us. With a feeling of relief I realized the uproar of tank engines and steel treads grinding on pavement had masked the sound of Joe's carbine. No other soldiers, particularly no officers or MPs, would come rushing to the scene to see why a shot had been fired.

We marched off down the street, side by side, two sturdy representatives of the law and order that Americans would maintain in the captured cities of Germany.

We must have stayed in that town for several days as I remember two instances of interaction between our troops and people of the town.

Two of our men, cheerful, college boy types, walking along a street, fell in behind a trio of attractive young women. The women glanced back at them then studiously ignored them, walking on in silence. Of course the men were under orders not to fraternize with Germans, but soon one of them began to speculate, rather loudly, about the possibility of becoming acquainted with the Frauleins. The women continued to ignore them. After a while the talkative American, convinced that the girls could not understand him, began to speculate about the probable sexual behavior of German women. His companion apparently found this amusing and added some of his own thoughts on the subject, but suddenly one of the girls stopped, turned around and began to denounce her annoyers in perfect English. She declared she would never have any kind of association with the barbaric Americans who were known to be stealing everything they could get their hands on and generally behaving as badly as the terrible Russians who were looting and burning Eastern Germany. At least the two young men were embarrassed and tried to apologize for their behavior. Then they turned and beat a hasty retreat from the scene.

Another situation which I witnessed, involved an actual struggle between a German girl and one of our own for possession of a radio which our man had "confiscated." I was with a group of soldiers who were waiting to cross a street when we became aware that one of our medics, a rather chubby corporal, was coming toward us, walking fast, carrying a mantle radio of the well-known Philco style—like a wooden box with a arched top and a little window on the front through which the number of the station could be seen. Coming up behind him at a run was a German girl—a tall blonde with an athletic form and a pretty face. Just as the corporal arrived adjacent to our group the girl caught up wit him and seized the radio, trying to pull it from his grip. He struggled to retain his hold and this led to a man versus woman wrestling match in which the two contestants were locked together, each with arms firmly wrapped around the radio, each wrenching vigorously at the prize in an effort to jerk it from the grip of the other. It was soon evident that while the corporal had a considerable weight advantage, it was the girl who was physically fit and ready for a contest of this kind. She was shouting, in good English, exclamations like, "You will not take my radio!" with no evidence that she was winded, while the fat corporal was red of face and grunting noisily with each futile heave. This struggle could have lasted for a while longer but there were angry mutterings coming from the crowd of watching soldiers. Though all of these men presumably knew that we had been ordered to confiscate civilian radios, they were now expressing sympathy for the girl. An attractive young woman, dressed like an American college girl in sweater and skirt with sensible shoes for walking, simply did not register in our minds as an enemy. I was not surprised therefore when the big wreaker driver, Buba, came forward from the group growling "Give 'er that radio!"

His threatening aspect apparently shook the corporal's concentration and caused him to loosen his grip. The girl darted away, hugging the radio to her bosom, running back in the direction from which she had come. The corporal did not acknowledge the presence of Sergeant Bubba or any of us with so much as a glance. He simply turned away, red faced and breathing hard, and walked off in a direction opposite to that which the girl had taken.

How the non-fraternization policy was supposed to work was never explained to us in detail. Word spread that any effort to make friends with a German, particularly one of the opposite sex, was absolutely forbidden. We assumed at first that any commercial contacts, such as buying from stores, restaurants, or the beer joints that sprang up in houses near our billets, were also forbidden, but a curious contradiction of this appeared on payday: Soldiers salaries, always paid in cash, were suddenly being paid in crisp, newly printed German Marks. If we were denied all contact with civilians then how were we to spend our money? Obviously brief commercial contacts, such as the purchase of a bottle of schnapps, did not constitute fraternization. This raised an interesting question for some: Could a soldier visit and pay a prostitute without fraternizing? I never heard how this was resolved.

Years later I learned that this freshly printed money represented a government policy designed to save enormous costs to the occupying powers. The money was printed by the allies, the Germans were required by law (Allied Military Law) to accept it at face value, and it was used not only for soldier's salaries but much more extensively to buy bulk supplies for the army of occupation. Presumably this meant our food had a local source. The German farms remained productive, in spite of the manpower shortage, and it was certainly more efficient for the army to buy food on the local markets than to ship it from overseas. One evidence that we saw of this was the sudden appearance of ersatz coffee. This substitute "coffee" was produced from roasted grain and had been a standard feature of German cuisine during the war years. We considered it practically undrinkable and I personally formed the habit of loading my cup with several spoonfuls of sugar and a large addition of canned milk to conceal its taste. You may be sure the result bore no resemblance to a cup of Brazilian coffee and of course it contained no stimulating caffeine.

Reference material that is now available states that this "state sponsored counterfeiting scheme" (if one may dare to call it that) saved the United States many billions of dollars. Our printing presses rolled, spewing out marks, and the Germans were in no position to object—least of all the German farmers who were getting good prices for their grain and potatoes.

CHAPTER 26

BEYOND THE RHINE

In the sparse journal I was able to keep, March 28 is recorded as a date we were "on the road" all night. I believe we were in a line of trucks, many miles long, that was slowly edging its way toward a pontoon bridge across the Rhine. In any case, we did cross the Rhine the next day in the vicinity of the German city of Worms. The bridge, constructed by engineers, was far south of the well known bridge at Remagen where the first crossing of the Rhine had been accomplished by seventh army infantry about three weeks earlier. After crossing, out battalion—or at least Headquarters Company— camped in a sheep pasture on the east side of the river. Our camp site will probably be remembered by any of the men who slept there—perhaps I should say, tried to sleep there—as the sound of artillery shells passing high overhead was almost continuous. I try to remember what the sound was like—someone said it was a tearing, ripping sound as if the shells were tearing their way through the air. Someone else said it was like the sound of a car racing very fast over a gravel road. Our big guns were lined up along the west bank of the Rhine, firing across the river and over our heads at targets far to the east. The artillery units at this time possessed detailed military maps of the German roads. These were so precise the big guns could drop their shells on road junctions and other critical targets miles away.

It was very dark in the field which may have been lit only by starlight, or perhaps the sky was overcast. Whichever, our eyes adapted so we could see one another as shadowy figures and avoid stepping on those who were already in their sleeping bags on the ground. As I was preparing my own sleeping bag, shots were heard over on one side of the field. Single shots, widely spaced, were being fired. These were identifiable as coming from a small weapon, probably a hand gun. Several men began to move towed the sound to investigate. The shooter was soon located—a lone man standing beside a sheep. As we approached he pointed a hand gun at the head of the animal and fired. The sheep collapsed, and as we came closer we recognized the sheep killer as our own master sergeant of the motor pool. He announced, "These sheep are sick and I'm putting them out of their misery." Not a likely story, I thought. He's killing them because he likes to kill things. The other possibility, suggested during a later discussion of the incident, was that if he had once been a cowboy, as he claimed, he may simply have been expressing his hatred for sheep. (Everybody who watched the western movies of those days believed that cowboys hate sheepherders and their sheep)

I have another memory of that night. Guard duty was arranged in a somewhat informal manner. I was to be one of the guards, and the man who had the shift before mine was supposed to awaken me when his time was finished. I awoke about an hour after I should been awakened, looked at my watch and was shocked to discover that I had been sleeping during the time I was supposed to be on guard duty. I leaped up and instantly assumed the aspect of an alert guard. Why I was not awakened by the man who was responsible was a matter I thought it better not to inquire about. Either he, or the man before him, had failed in their duty, but if this became known, the guilty party might try to protect his own skin by claiming he had awakened me and I must have gone back to sleep. Going to sleep while on guard duty was a very serious offense, especially in a combat zone. Not many years ago soldiers were executed for dozing off while on gurd duty. I seem to recall Abraham Lincoln intervened to save a young soldier who as to be executed for this offence.

Soon after that we moved on to the city of Wurzbutrg and had a good meal at a transient kitchen that had been set up in a palace. We sat on the steps of a magnificent staircase eating the food in our mess kits and gazing at pictures on the walls of a great hall. I recall a picture of a dog which seemed to be half out of the picture frame as if it were standing on the floor of a balcony with only the upper half of its body inside the frame and a human leg extending out of another picture as if the subject were emerging from the painted scene into real life. Most of the decorations, everything from columns of marble of an unusual color to fantastic carvings were too complex to persist in my memory. Some of this art seemed pornographic, at least to soldiers, with naked figures clinging to one another. After lunch we prowled about the grounds and I became convinced that a fire fight had occurred around the building in which many soldiers had been killed. There were large pools of blood on the ground where the bodies of wounded men had lain. German rifles were scattered about that had been deliberately ruined by swinging them against trees to bend the barrels. Strangely, a number of dead squirrels were lying on the ground. We looked through windows into a flooded basement where gruesome forms were floating in the water. The whole area had a chilling effect on my imagination. Surely, terrible things had happened here.

Years later, when I traveled as a tourist, retracing my wartime journey through Germany, I sought out the palace, which I now learned was called "Die Residenz," and revisited the grounds as well as the interior. In a nearby shop I talked to a German woman who had been a resident of the city at the time of its capture and had later worked for the American Military government there. She cleared up the mystery of "The Residence" at once. The building had been used by the Americans as a field hospital. So many wounded men had been brought to the place many had lain on the grass outside while waiting for attention. Wounded German soldiers were treated also. Their abandoned rifles were swung against trees to bend the barrels so they could no longer be fired. . The squirrels were shot by American soldiers "for fun," she said.

The next day we moved on to the big city of Mannheim. It was our first experience of the destruction visited on German cities by so called carpet bombing. I remember the scene in one location near the center of the city where whole blocks of buildings had been reduced to piles of bricks and masonry. Our engineer bulldozers had made a new road through the rubble. It seemed to me at one point the road did not follow a former street—which would have been completely hidden from the bulldozer drivers—but had cut through the middle of blocks. We heard gunfire nearby. Our infantry had not yet cleared all of the enemy soldiers from the city. It seemed likely such hold out soldiers were volkstrum units that had been ordered to hold where they were posted days before and who had received no notice that their stand was futile.

A few days earlier we had still been west of the Rhine with Mannheim in the distance and I had written a letter in which I said: "Across the river, a city with a fierce Teutonic name lies dead under a shroud of gray smoke." I never learned if that bit of whimsy made it past the censor.

CHAPTER 27

MESSERSCHMITTS!

Most civilized people would be shocked the first time they see dead people lying on the ground. But of course, war does strange things to soldier's minds. In a sense, enemy soldiers are no longer regarded as human. The death of an enemy is not a tragedy, it is a good thing, it makes my own life and the lives of my companions safer. This is an instinct, I believe, that dates back to the long millennia of savagery when "kill or be killed" was natures law for primitive tribesman.

Our convoy was rolling east on a bright day in the first week of April and we were sharing a lunch in the back of a truck. We had opened cans of frankfurters and beans, our favorite among canned rations, and were eating a cold lunch, washed down by the water from our canteens. We passed a German gun emplacement, a pit dug in the soil of a field near the road, surrounded by an embankment of the dirt that had been shoveled out of the pit. The pit may have held an antiaircraft or anti-tank gun but was now empty. Ling in a circle as if they had been blown out of the pit in various directions were the bodies of a half dozen soldiers in the *feldgrau* German uniforms. I suppose everyone in our truck stopped eating, but only for a moment. Someone said, "Well, those sonsofbitches got what they had coming!" and we resumed digging into our cans of frankfurters and beans.

Soon after that we saw the first dead horses. These had been big, handsome horses but their bodies were now bloated and torn with terrible wounds. It seemed evident they had been killed on the road, then pushed off the roar onto the shoulder. There were exclamations of pity and anger from the men in the truck. Someone said these were horses that had been seized from nearby farmers to pull trucks that had run out of gas, but this was only a guess and probably wrong. I later learned that the German army had always used horses to pull supply wagons, even as they boasted of having a super-modern motorized army. And these horses had been killed by our night-flying pilots who at this stage of the war were actually patrolling roads back of the enemy lines. They flew just high enough to clear the treetops and fired at any shadowy forms that could be seen on the road below. Our planes still flew at speeds well below the speed of sound, so the soldiers on the road could hear them coming and seek shelter in roadside ditches or run furiously away into the fields. But the horses, hitched to wagons, made big targets that could not avoid the bullets or exploding shells from a plane. We saw many dead horses that day and I think most of my companions were disturbed by the sight. In those days, all American children, even in cities where live horses were seldom seen, saw and admired horses in the many western movies. There were even well-known super horses of certain celebrities—such as Trigger, the horse of Roy Rogers, that performed amazing feats of intelligence on screen that no doubt left children believing horses are almost as smart as their human companions. Sophisticates might sneer at such films as "Horse Operas," but children yearned for ponies and dreamed of riding with cowboys in the wide open spaces of the west.   Buba was still in a rage that evening, cursing those "damned Germans" who had exposed the horses to the dangers of war.

Shortly after that, on another April morning, we had our only experience with the almost extinct German air force. Riding eastward in the back of a truck we suddenly became aware of the steady thump, thump, thump, of a forty millimeter Bofors gun firing nearby. This was the superb antiaircraft gun originally developed by the Swedes in cooperation with the British but later manufactured in large numbers in the USA and Canada as well as in England.

Our truck came to a halt. Someone was shouting. It was Spode. He was running down the road shoulder yelling, "Get out of the trucks! Get out of the trucks!" We did so in a wild scramble, tumbling over the end gate, falling in the road, leaping up and running furiously across the shallow roadside ditch and out into the adjacent field. There was a sort of mound or low hillock in the middle of the field and everyone from my truck seemed to have the same ides—to throw himself down on the side of the mound away from the planes. More antiaircraft guns were firing now, their shells bursting high overhead like fireworks. I was suddenly aware that my helmet had been left behind in the truck. I had worn that hated bucket every day since landing in France. Now for the first time I needed it; my head felt naked under the threat of steel splinters falling from the bursting shells. We could see the planes now. They seemed to be circling us in a broad circle, perhaps a mile across. I recall vividly their shape—black silhouettes against the brightness of the sky—exactly like those in the training films on aircraft identification. Voices around me were calling out their ugly name: Messerschmitts! As we lay prone on the ground, lifting our heads only enough to watch them, they gathered into a loose formation and came racing along the highway back of our convoy. Their guns—probably 20 millimeter aircraft canon—started firing with a thunderous roar. We could see they were targeting the tank column which our trucks had passed just before the first Bofors was heard. Before they reached the hindmost truck in our stalled convoy, which incidentally was the explosives truck with its dangerous cargo for our demolitions men, they stopped firing—or ran out of ammunition—and broke out of their formation to scatter all over the sky that was now decorated by the puffy white clouds left behind by exploding flack from the Bofors.

At this point we were startled anew by the bang, bang ,bang of a semi-automatic weapon right there in our midst. It was Joe, lying on his back firing at the sky with his thirty caliber carbine. This was a weapon that, it was generally agreed, would make a good rabbit gun provided the rabbit was standing still and not too far away. Firing it at fighter planes streaking across the sky was about as effective as throwing rocks or yelling curses. But one of the planes was streaming a plume of black smoke as it disappeared into the distance. Joe rose up screaming, "I hit it! I hit it!"

We walked back to the trucks laughing at the absurdity of his claim. We pointed out that an unknown number of anti-aircraft guns had been firing at the planes and if a plane was hit it was one of them that had hit it. But Joe believed what he wanted to believe and I am sure if you asked his grandchildren today what Grandpa Joe did in the Great War they would tell you he shot down a German plane.

Before we reached the road the column of tanks came lumbering along, passing the parked trucks of our convoy. They showed no evidence of damage. Officers were standing up in the turrets, gazing at the sky where the puffs of white smoke were fading away. We wondered why the commander of the aircraft had chosen to bounce the small twenty millimeter shells harmlessly off the heavily armored tanks instead of striking our convoy. That burst of cannon fire could have wreaked and burned many trucks and injured or killed some soldiers. We were, of course, thankful for the outcome of this adventure. I was thankful that Spode didn't notice my helmet was missing as I walked back to the truck.

CHAPTER 28

THE OTHER ARMY

Our convoys always traveled at a sedate speed, probably about thirty five miles per hour. That was the speed I heard repeated as the top speed for army vehicles though I never had cause to check it or, not being a driver, to maintain it. On a long day trip, speed was not increased in order to complete the journey sooner, instead the travel plan simply called for more time on the road, even extending into the night, in order to cover the prescribed distance. After a few weeks on the roads of Germany, it became apparent that one group of drivers were consistently exceeding the speed limit. These speeders were not driving in a convoy; they were individual truckers of the supply service (Quartermaster Corps.)

We came to believe these drivers were exempt from the usual army rules of the road. As we crawled along in convoy they passed us as if they were driving high performance sport cars. They seemed to be taking reckless chances. They seemed to be free of supervision. In small towns as we passed through we saw them taking breaks, two men together, always African-Americans, sometimes talking and laughing in the company of German women. Once I saw one of their trucks racing along the road with a man pointing a pistol out of the right hand window to the consternation of officers in a jeep the truck was passing. It seemed to us that these men of the supply service had been given free rein to go hell for leather and damn the rules so long as the supplies got through!

It also seemed to be an example of the segregation which was maintained in the army of that day. All of the men of our battalion were white. Group pictures of my colleagues show not even a Latino among us. But we knew there were engineer units composed entirely of black enlisted men under the command of white officers. It was generally believed such units were used for heavy labor, pick and shovel work, road and airport builders. The Motor officer we called Sad Sack had finally been transferred to such a unit. He had been summoned from his gentleman-of-leisure life with us to an interview with superior officers. He had been asked (according to his own account) if he had had any experience in commanding black troops. He had answered (again, according to his own account of the interview,) that he had been "treated like a Niger" ever since he had joined our outfit! We found it scarcely believable that he had responded in this way to a group of superior officers who were in the act of deciding his future. But I considered it noteworthy that he confided in us, a few of the enlisted men he had previously ignored, as if seeking sympathy. He left us and we heard later that he had been injured while riding in a jeep that hit a mine.

Much later, after returning to the states, I was assigned to teach in an automotive school where some of my classes were composed entirely of African Americans. Like the white soldiers in my classes, they were men who had been auto mechanics in civilian life or who had scored high on the mechanical aptitude test. Their discipline was excellent. They sat in their seats tense and alert on the first day, examining me with expressions that can best be described as wary. They soon loosened up. During the breaks I joined in their conversations, laughed at their rough humor and treated them as equals in spite of the intimidating stripes on my sleeve. Soon they were confiding in me about the terrible treatment they were receiving from their training sergeant. They described him as a huge black man with lots of stripes on his sleeve and a voice so loud it could almost knock a man down. The punishments he doled out to those who made mistakes in marching, or in work details seemed unbelievable. And he was much devoted to punishing the whole platoon of forty-eight men for the mistakes of individuals. One day they all seemed sleepy. During the first break period they told me how the sergeant had rousted them out of bed at two A M and ordered them to assemble in the street outside the barracks for a roll call. They were given just a few minutes to dress in O D uniforms with neckties and steel helmets and, as an added indignity, each man had to carry his footlocker out of the building and stack it with the others in a neat pile on the lawn between the barracks and the street. Other punishment sessions had involved scrubbing the floor of the barracks and adjacent latrine at some ungodly hour like four A M. When I asked if an officer was supervising the sergeant who was making their lives miserable, they indicated that they almost never saw an officer.

In spite of this harassment, that may have been widespread among black troops, they introduced a new tradition to the army. Ours was said to be the silent army; we marched with only the cadence count of platoon sergeants. We never sang. Older American armies had been known for their singing on the march. Revolutionary war soldiers marched to the sound of fifes and drums, singing of Yankee Doodle. Soldiers of the Mexican War, singing a popular song of the day—Green Grow the Lilacs where my true love lies sleeping—are believed to have added a new word, "Gringo" to the Mexican language. And the soldiers of the Civil War sang "The Battle Hymn of the Republic" or "Dixie" depending on their patriotic inclination. But the American soldiers of world war two, bouncing on the hard seats of trucks rushing them to battle had little inclination to sing. But now as the army moved toward integration and trained more and more black troops, the chanting of sergeants took on a more musical sound and at a shout of "Sound off!" the whole troop would roar rhythmically and melodically something like the "Jodie chant":

> "Tain't no use in goin home.
> Jodie's got your girl and gone!"

Soon many different chants were taking the place of the monotonous "one, two, Three, four" of training sergeants and the U S Arny became musical again.

CHAPTER 29

BED CHECK CHARLEY

April 8, 1945. This was almost exactly one month prior to V E Day. Patton's tanks were somewhere far to the East but we were unaware of the nearness of victory. We were aware of the rumor that Hitler was about to spring some surprise, a new attack larger then the Bulge, or some terrible secret weapon that would devastate our armies. Of course, the rumor originated in the Nazi propaganda mill that was still assuring the German public that their country cold not possibly be defeated by the inferior Slavs and the American gangsters.

We were billeted in a small farm village where residents had been expelled from their houses and directed to live in their barns while we were among them. Typically, barns and outhouses were grouped around a central courtyard paved with cobblestones. As we were moving into the house assigned to us, a *hausfrau* stood in the courtyard outside her barn door and cried out that God was punishing her for her sins by sending the soldiers to expel here from her home. Harry, always ready to share his understanding of the German language, translated what she was saying, and probably violated the rule against fraternization by telling her we would be there for only a few days. It seemed to me her grief over being required to sleep in the barn was unreasonable. Not far away, city dwellers had experienced nights of terror, destruction of their homes, and death of loved ones in the massive air raids that destroyed large areas of German cities. Here the houses of this small village were undamaged and our soldiers would do no ham to the buildings and furniture we were using for a short time. We slept under duvets, those European comforters like giant pillows, and had our evening bull-sessions while seated on comfortable chairs. I had a private room with a bed that was too short for me and a table on which I placed my liberated typewriter and wrote letters home.

Lured by the comfortable bed, I retired early and was soon shocked awake by the blare of German martial music. I recognized the tune as a favorite marching song for Nazi parades that I had heard in newsreels back home. Now it blasted me awake with the rattle of tenor drums and the clash of hobnail boots on pavement. I was scrambling in the dark to find my carbine before I realized the music had the discordance of the old, non-electronic phonographs and was coming, not from the street outside, but from downstairs. Now that I was wide awake I realized that one of my night-owl companions, in the downstairs living room, had decided to wind up the family phonograph and listen to some German music.

I suppose this experience reinforced in my mind the rumor that Hitler was going to stage a surprise that would change the course of the war. In any case I went back to sleep with my carbine beside me on the bed. I was awakened at dawn by the master sergeant opening my door and starting to yell one of his usual wake-up calls. ("Rise and shine!" is the only non-obscene one I remember). In this instance he saw the carbine on my bed and yelled a profanity followed by "I'm goanna get my head blown of some morning by one of you nervous bastards." I took this to mean I was not the only one sharing his bed with a lethal weapon.

One afternoon I entered the courtyard and found the German housewife standing outside the barn door with her face animated by a delighted smile. She was watching Earl Stroud who was leaning out of her kitchen window and watering the bright red geraniums in the window box. She beamed at me, pointed to him and said, "Es gipt einen gutten mann!"

A good man indeed for watering flowers, but about two hours later I saw the shocked expression on her face when she caught him emerging from her barn with a large container full of stolen potatoes. She said nothing, just stared, and he pretended not to see her. He had decided to prepare an evening feast of potatoes, sliced and fried in real lard, as a break from our usual army chow. He fired up the wood-burning range in her kitchen and carried out this project so expertly a rumor spread among his comrades that he had once been a professional cook.

I think it was in this village that we began to receive our nightly visits from Bed Check Charley. This was our nickname for the observation plane that came over every night, passing so high in the sky it was invisible against the background of stars. Its engines went zoom-zoom-zoom. I had first heard that sound in war movies where the American planes always had a steady, smooth sound and the enemy aircraft always went zoom-zoom-zoom. Now here it was in real life—German planes really did sound like that!

The explanation was simple: It was a two-engine plane and the engines were not synchronized to run at exactly the same speed. Sound waves of almost the same frequency from two different sources alternately reinforce and interfere with one another producing what physicists call a "beat." So, night after night, the beat of two unsynchronized aircraft engines called us out of our blacked-out houses to stare up at the sky. I don't believe anyone in our outfit ever actually saw Bed Check Charley. Since he never dropped a bomb, or otherwise behaved as a threat, we finally learned to disregard him. He was just looking, though what he could have been looking for while flying over a completely blacked-out landscape well behind the front remained a mystery. I remember waking in the night and hearing the throbbing rhythm up in the sky. It would lull me back to sleep like the sound of a distant train in my childhood.

The memory of the sound is associated with another small village where I had a private room in a farmhouse. Here, for some unknown reason, the farmer and his wife were allowed to remain in the house. As I came and went they greeted me with serious, respectful expressions on their faces as if I were a welcome guest. Every day the woman made up my bed and tidied my room. There were pictures on the walls of young men in military uniforms. A patriotic family, I thought, until someone explained that these were portraits awarded to the parents of soldiers who had died in combat. I wondered about the attitude of my erstwhile hosts who appeared to be kindly disposed toward an enemy soldier after having lost their own sons in war. Had their young men been killed on the Russian front? Were their sons secret pacifists who had opposed the war but could not avoid being drafted into the army? Were they simply grieving parents who, with the wisdom of their loss, could see any young soldier as the son of people who, like themselves, were trapped in the grip of an implacable war machine, blameless for what was symbolized by the uniform. Since I was under orders not to converse with Germans, I would never know their story.

In this same village Harry had found temporary happiness in another house where he could be alone with his books and his current literary project. He was still translating a French novel into English. The weather was warm now and windows could be left open to admit the afternoon breeze, or in his case the overpowering stench of manure piled against the stone wall of the house under his window. I went over to see him one evening but stayed only a few minutes. He commented, "It's the only time I've had any privacy since I joined the army."

The cultural gap between typical Americans and German farmers showed itself in other ways. One day I was with a few other men who looked out of the back window of a farmhouse and witnessed a shocking scene. A farmer was holding a lamb in his arms as if posing in the guise of Saint Francis of Assisi. The lamb had a puppy-like face and bright, alert eyes. He put the lamb down on the ground so it was standing beside him then bent over it, restraining it with one hand. His other hand held a knife. The farmer cut its throat and it stood there wagging its tail vigorously like a small white dog as its blood streamed out. Finally its legs buckled and it sank to the ground and died.

One of the watching soldiers began to curse, "these damned Germans," as if he thought the killing of a lamb was further evidence of the evil of the Nazis. Needless to say, most Americans have never witnessed the killing of animals that provide the meat on their dinner tables. For a European farmer, killing a lamb is simply one of the skills handed down from his ancestors—a simple farm task having no emotional or moral significance, but to an American boy from a big city it was a shocking example of brutal cruelty.

We stayed in that village for several days. I rigged a bedside light for reading using a spare truck battery and a headlight bulb. This worked fine for an hour or so but unfortunately a faulty blackout curtain allowed a sliver of light to escape. Heavy footsteps thumped in the hallway outside my door and Captain T. burst in shouting, "Douse that light!"

Since rules of military courtesy did not spell out the proper reaction for a soldier reading in bed who is suddenly confronted by an irate Officer of The Day, I simply pulled a wire loose from the battery, plunging the room into total darkness. The captain found the door and slammed it as he left. Then there was a loud noise from the dark hallway. I think he stumbled over a piece of furniture he had somehow avoided on the way in. I lay there wondering, without much concern, if I could be disciplined for my unauthorized use of a truck battery and a headlight bulb. It seemed unlikely. As an electrician I had several times rigged unorthodox lights for the officer's and had recently been praised by the motor officer for building a battery charger from junk parts. This same motor officer still believed I could carry out a completely impractical idea he had dreamed up: to install powerful electro-magnets under the trucks to pick up nails off the road before they found their way into the tires of our vehicles. When driving past buildings that had been shattered by bombs, old nails scattered on the roadway were a real problem. I had managed to stall on that project for weeks—impossible to find the necessary parts, and impossible to provide the power for such an arrangement even if it was built. Fortunately the war was almost over.

In another village, where we stayed for a few nights, illegal fraternization became almost flagrant. In an evening bull session the conversation was dominated by talk about the local farm girls. I noted that the men who were discussing this topic most knowledgably were dressed in their best O D uniforms and were smoothly shaved. Some of them wafted the fragrance of cologne or after-shave lotion. In the absence of barber shops, they had been giving one another haircuts, usually with rather poor results. It was evident they were seeking romantic liaisons and had, or shall I say claimed to have had, some success in this endeavor. Buba, the big wreaker driver, was particularly boastful about his conquests. Though he was never seen to carry or use a phrase book he had somehow picked up the essentials of the local dialect in a very short time. When I mentioned this to Harry he said that Low German was no doubt closely related to illiterate English. And he pointed out that it doesn't take too many words to persuade a girl, if she likes the man's looks and he has a nice smile. As for me I found the local farm girls unappealing. They had pleasant faces and ready smiles but they were broad of beam and their muscular legs were often quite hairy.

CHAPTER 30

THE FINAL COLLAPSE

Now the terror that has haunted the dreams of Germans for centuries had become real. The uncountable hordes of the Slavs, the merciless Cossacks, the brutal tartars and dart Turkmen from the boundless steppes of the east had been loosed to plunder, rape and murder defenseless Germans. There was a plaintive outcry on the radio that "The homes of cultured Germans are being looted and burned. Gentle and innocent German girls are being raped by filthy Mujiks. The purity of the German race is being destroyed. There is nothing to do but flee, and nowhere to flee but to the west. The Americans are civilized. (Last week they were gangsters!) Only they can save the German people from the Tartar Hordes."

I wrote in a letter: Now the road we travel is an escape route for pitiful people who have nothing but the clothes on their backs. Families from the Eastern parts of Germany are fleeing by any means they can manage in an effort to find some sanctuary beyond reach of the advancing Russians. Sometimes they are pushing carts with a few household belongings. Sometimes they are in wagons pulled by gaunt horses—whole families, women and children, riding slowly toward the west. We see a man pushing a cart containing a woman—a pregnant woman with a very large belly; her time is soon. Most amazing of all, German Soldiers without weapons are walking toward the west. They are looking for someone to surrender to—an American soldier, of course.

We saw American army trucks carrying German prisoners who were sitting on the hoods of the vehicles with their feet resting on the front bumper. I saw one truck with three Germans sitting side by side on the hood in this manner. We remarked that the driver of the truck must have difficulty seeing the road ahead.

Buba and Earl, on a mission in the wreaker, encountered a starved-looking German soldier who was standing beside the road, trying to get their attention, holding his hands up in a signal of surrender. They stopped, gave him something to eat, then had him sit on the hood of the truck in the manner they had observed with the other prisoners. I suspect they saw this as a novel adventure they could tell us about later. However they found they had to drive very slowly to keep the weakened man from falling off, so they started thinking of how they could get rid of him in an acceptable way. They drove into a Military Police check point and asked what to do with their prisoner. The sergeant on duty said, "Take the son of a bitch down the road, run him into the woods and shoot him."

Buba thought the MP was joking but when he responded honestly, "We can't do that," an M. P. officer standing nearby rapped, "That's an order, do what the sergeant says."

Buba was apparently too shocked to say anything at this point, but Earl, perceiving that the solution to the standoff was to declare their willingness to comply, said, "We'll do it, sir!" They drove on down the road until they were out of sight of the MPs but still close enough for a gun shot to be heard. They got their "prisoner" off of the truck, shooed him into the woods, and then Earl pointed his carbine at the sky and fired several quick rounds. After that they drove away, fast.

This was of course after the incidents at Malmedy, during the Battle of the Bulge, when Americans who had been captured were execute by SS troops. There were several incidents during the battle in which the Germans herded American prisoners into a field and fired machine guns into the crowd. Americans who were wounded and fell, and some who were unhurt but pretended they were dead, were executed by gunshots to the head. It certainly was not reported in the news that Americans later retaliated in kind.

Somewhat later Earl got a chance to actually fire a gun at an enemy—or so he thought. Our convoy stopped for a while in a small village and as the other men spilled out of their trucks into the street to stretch their legs, Earl climbed up into the turret back of the cab where a fifty caliber machine gun was mounted. There had been talk that it was a ridiculous place to mount a machine gun since anyone who manned it would be perched up there in full view of any enemy that he could see and shoot at. I had never seen the gun fired and had no idea who, if anyone in our group, was assigned to man it. Certainly Earl was one of the least likely among us to yearn for glory in combat. He was one of the older men, at least thirty five. He was also thought to be a very level-headed person. But on this day he was up there in the turret, inspecting or tinkering with some part of the mechanism, when a noisy, single-engine plane came zooming over the housetops to pass right above our heads. From its shape and noise, most of us knew instantly it was one of our own small observation planes that offered no threat to persons on the ground. Unbelievably, Earl started firing. Lunging from one side of the turret to the other, he seemed to be tracking the plane across the sky. Fortunately he had received no training on the weapon and I suppose his chance of hitting the fast-moving target was close to zero. As the deafening sound of the gun lapsed into ear-ringing silence, someone yelled, "You idiot! That was one of ours!"

Earl responded, almost calmly, "Didn't you see the black crosses on the wings?"

This brought a howl of protest from his audience. In the uproar of voices the prevailing opinion was obvious: the plane had white stars on its wings. Someone yelled, "Since when do the Krauts fly Piper Cubs?"

This matter was never resolved. Earl declared he saw German markings on the plane. Never mind that the rest of us were sure it was American. He held firmly to what he thought he had seen and seemed puzzled that the rest of us could be so wrong. Let the psychologists explain what happened in his mind in that instant when he, with his hands on a powerful weapon, saw a plane coming toward him threateningly. Curiously, no officer came to investigate the sound of the firing. Certainly no enlisted man would have informed those in command of such a matter. It became a secret, remembered but seldom mentioned by the men who witnessed it.

Later it occurred to me that this incident was simply a prank. Earl had been itching to fire the gun and had simply pointed it at the sky—not at the plane—and fired a few rounds. I tried to get him to confess, confidentially, that this was so, but he insisted again that he had really seen those black Maltese crosses on the plane's wings.

CHAPTER 31

FREEDOM FOR PRISONERS

Now the good news had been confirmed. Hitler's thousand-year Reich had collapsed. There had been an official surrender. Though the members of the Nazi hierarchy, who had inherited the torch of leadership from Hitler, had tried to surrender only to the Americans and British, this had not been allowed. Only unconditional surrender would be accepted and of course this included surrender to the Russians as well.

The American and French forces continued to move toward the possible Alpine redoubt. It was still believed that diehard Nazis might make a stand in the Bavarian Alps even after they received word of an official surrender. Another explanation for our continuing travel to the south-east may have been the difficulty of changing travel orders for such a huge numbers of troops, all moving in accordance with a detailed plan.

One day our convoy stopped beside a small town park and we spilled out of the trucks, glad to escape from the hard wooden seats for at least a few minutes and to stretch our legs by walking about. It was a fine day. Though it was May, the breeze, here in the northern foothills of the Alps, had the feeling of a first warm day in spring.

Something of interest was happening in the park. Housewives were scurrying about, putting food on a long table under the trees. They were chattering excitedly to one another as they worked. Of more professional interest to us, a formation of men in the *feldgrau* uniforms of German soldiers was assembled at the far end of the park. They were facing away from us, facing a few American officers who seemed to be conferring around a small table. Drawn by curiosity, we moved closer, and stood back of the German formation, watching. There was something very odd about these soldiers. Some of them were remarkably small, five feet or less, I thought. Many of the taller ones had fringes of gray or white hair showing beneath the edges of their forage caps. All of them were very thin

An American officer came forward from the group around the table and called out *"Achtung!"*. The smaller soldiers stiffened to rigid attention, but some of the tall ones were stooped with rounded shoulders and presented a very unmilitary appearance. We knew at once this was the *volkstrum*, the Peoples Army, that final draft of old men and boys with no qualifications for military service beyond the ability to carry some sort of weapon. They represented the last reserves of manpower in a nation bled white by the slaughter on the Russian Front and in Italy and France. They had been called to defend a desperate nation faced with inevitable defeat. Harry muttered "My God, just little boys and old men,"

Joe said, "They should have drafted the women. Those farm girls that we saw loading hay onto a wagon would have made better soldiers than this bunch."

Somebody else said, "Whose side are you on, Joe? If they'd drafted the women we wouldn't get home till nineteen fifty five."

There may have been some truth in this. Much later I learned that at Stalingrad, Russian women who had been assigned to man the antiaircraft guns had joined in the battle on an equal footing with men. Lowering the muzzles of their guns they fired point blank at the German tanks and kept firing until they died. German soldiers at Stalingrad were shocked to learn that they had been fighting against women. Hitler, we know, ordained that women should confine themselves to children, cooking and church.

Now roll was being called. The American officer was reading names from a list. Little boys, whose voices had not changed, were answering shrilly. Old men were responding gruffly. Each came forward and was given an official looking piece of paper, then left the formation and went into the park, dashing or hobbling as they were able.

Joe exclaimed, "Those lucky bastards!" They're getting discharged from the army!"

They came past us, some faces happy with sudden freedom, others blank, emotionless. Some were scanning their discharge papers as if finding it hard to believe they were real. Some stuffed folded papers into their pockets without looking at them. All were converging on the long table where the food was waiting. I reflected that these German women, knowing the American army only through slanderous propaganda, probably thought this would be the first good food their men had tasted since their capture. I thought to myself that in a few days those men and boys will be remembering good GI chow with longing.

On a map of south Germany I can pick out the names of a few towns where we stayed overnight, but I cannot remember the location of a few memorable or tragic events that occurred. For example there was the demise of one of the cooks. He was unloading supplies from the back of a truck when the driver decided to back the vehicle close to the loading platform. The unlucky man fell under one of the rear wheels that rolled over him. He died at the scene.

A technician from the recon unit, whose name I have forgotten, found a German anti-tank rocket lying in a field. It appeared to be a version of our well-known bazooka—the shoulder launched rocket that all of us had been trained to fire. For the amusement of his companions, he hoisted the German *Panzerfast* to his shoulder and fired it toward an empty field. There must have been some significant difference in design or in training of soldiers using the device, for the man was badly burned by the exhaust blast. He was shipped off to a hospital in Paris where he recovered and enjoyed a lengthy vacation. Curiously, through some fluke in paper work, he was awarded the Purple Heart Medal for having been injured by enemy fire.

There was another tragedy of a poignant nature. In one village where we stayed for a week or more, Harry (in clear violation of the non-fraternization rule) acquired a charming girl friend, a tall, pleasant-looking *fraulein* with long blonde hair and a sweet smile. They took long walks together, she practicing her English, he perfecting his German, or so he said.

But, of course, we had to move on, though in this case only about twenty miles to another village. After a few days Harry hitched a ride with one of the supply drivers who was going in the right direction and arrived at the front door of his erstwhile feminine companion. The girl's mother answered the door, took one look at Harry's smiling face and cried out, "Sie ist Todt" and began to sob and wail. When she regained control of her grief she explained that the very day we left the village the girl had begun to complain of a severe pain in her side. It was appendicitis. There was no doctor in the village and in the chaos of Germany's fall there was no means of transportation to another town. Our army doctors could have saved her, but the army had left. She had suffered great pain for several days, then died, presumably from a burst appendix and peritonitis.

CHAPTER 32

RUSSIANS AMONG US

As we continued to travel south in Bavaria we drove across a huge Air Base where enemy fighter planes were parked inside earth barriers meant to shield them from bombs exploding nearby. Mostly they were familiar types, Messerschmitts and Focke Wulf's but one of my companions became quite excited over one plane he had seen. He declared it had no propeller and was shaped more like a rocket than a typical plane. We had head rumors of a German rocket plane that could travel much faster then any of our fighters and theoretically had no ceiling. (How high it could climb was limited only by the amount of fuel it could carry.) This meant it could climb above any of our planes and then attack by diving down from a great height at tremendous speed. Apparently this was one of the miracle weapons that the Nazi propaganda mill had claimed would change the course of the war. Some sources claim at leas a thousand of these were built but most of our flyers never encountered one in the air. This late in the war German sources simply could not supply fuel for the new miracle weapons. Like the V2 rockets that fell on London, their main effect had been to distract a large segment of German industry into work that made no real contribution to winning the war.

Occasionally we stayed overnight in large cities, for example in Ulm on the Danube. We rolled across the famous river on a pontoon bridge and when the vehicle in which I was riding came to a temporary stop after the crossing, I used one frame of my precious film to take a picture of our last trucks rolling across. Cameras had been easy to come by; a large collection of confiscated cameras had been made available to us. I had chosen one to fit the only roll of P X film I had been able to buy at an earlier stop. It was a folding tourist camera. Expensive Leicas had gone to the first arrivals at the collection site—members of our recon group had done well for themselves, as had the battalion officers, but we of the ranks learned of the opportunity last and had to make do with cameras of lesser quality. The German civilians had been ordered to turn in all cameras, radios and firearms. Being a law aiding people they humbly delivered these designated items to the collection points. Of course a few rebellious youngsters, like the girl in a previous chapter who fought for her radio, resisted the order but the one collection site that I saw had a veritable hill of cameras stacked in a room of the town hall. I recall that one of our men who claimed to be politically savvy, declared that not only were these items being confiscated and destroyed but that factories which turned out such products were being "blown up." This, he said, was being done to boost the American post-war economy by creating a large demand for American cameras, guns and radios in Europe. Weather their was any truth in this I am not prepared to say and the politician types who spread such stories were rare. Most soldiers could not have cared less about such ideas.

The center of UIm had been flattened by bombs. The old stone bridges were down or at least rendered unusable and many city buildings had been reduced to mounds of bricks. But the great cathedral still stood, a towering structure, said to be the highest church in the world, at 530 feet it is comparable to the Washington monument. A magnificent tower, it was seemingly unaffected by the surrounding chaos until I came close enough to see that all the windows stared out hollow and empty of glass. Someone declared that it was customary to remove colored glass windows from such a structure to preserve them from being destroyed by nearby explosions but I can testify that I walked over ground beneath the walls that was carpeted by bits of colored glass. We were told the survival of the huge structure was evidence of the precision of our bombers. They had been ordered to preserve the great cathedrals as a treasure belonging to all humanity. If such an order was issued it must have been ignored. There is no reason to believe that, when a thousand planes flew over a large city and rained down missiles in the manner that was referred to as carpet bombing, one single structure could have been intentionally spared. It seems more reasonable to believe that the sheer massiveness of the cathedral saved it from destruction. I pocketed a small piece of red glass as a souvenir of the place and time.

Later that day while wandering the city streets we were astonished to see a Messerschmitt 109 flying high overhead. The plane, black against the blue sky and white clouds circled and dived erratically and was soon joined by another plane, a two-engine bomber. Both bore the Maltese cross of the Luftwaffe on their wings. There was an unreal feeling about this scene—pedestrians in the street ignored the planes and the French soldiers who were in evidence everywhere showed only a casual interest. An American M P, noting the surprise of my companions, told us that these were planes captured intact by our forces on a nearby German Air Base. Now they were being flown by *US* air corps pilots who had been assigned to the barracks of their erstwhile enemies. It was later said that the young flyers, bored by the sudden cessation of combat excitement, had turned with interest to examining the captured planes and then decided to see if they could fly them. This unauthorized sport was soon brought to a halt by an order handed down from higher command. This, it was said, after a fatal crash of one of the planes.

At one stop in a Bavarian village my companions and I shared a house with some Russian soldiers who had been adopted by Headquarters Company. Apparently there was a widespread but little known practice of assigning Russian prisoners, freed from German prison camps, to live with American outfits. The first of these could speak no English and so far as I know we had no Russian speaking interpreter in Headquarters Company. But I have a vivid memory of one Russian trying to tell us, in very poor English, about the tragic loss of most of his companions in the battle in which he had been captured. There was anguish in his voice and be began to cry. The sight of a grown man sobbing like a small boy who has been hurt, was shocking to us. It was widely believed in the nineteen forties that grown men did not cry. Sadly, the grief of the Russians among us was not over. It was widely believed that Joseph Stalin had no plans for rehabilitating the thousands of Russian prisoners the allies had freed. Much later it became known that Russians who had been captured by the Germans then rescued by the allies —and who were then turned over to the jurisdiction of the Russian army—were accused of having deserted and were executed. As in the Japanese army, no excuse was acceptable for having surrendered to the Enemy. Also it was widely believed that these Russians who had been "contaminated" by seeing the houses and towns of Western Europe and by seeing how American troops were housed and fed could not be trusted to fit in again in Russian society.

Soon after we left Ulm, a proclamation was posted on the company bulletin board that henceforth troops were to have their weekends off, free of duty. The order was signed by Dwight Eisenhower himself. I could not recall that I had seen his signature on our bulletin board before. Later I suspected that this may have been his first political ploy with his eye on the white house. Certainly he earned the thanks of a multitude of future voters with that gesture.

Sergeant Liberati had an exiting idea for our first free week-end. He would check out a company truck and drive to Italy. He said, "I really want to be able to write to my parents and tell them I was in Italy." So, with extra cans of gasoline on board, we headed south from Fussen, in Bavaria, and drove into Austria. We had no difficulties on the way to Innsbruck. MPs at checkpoints looked us over and waved us through. The mountain scenery was spectacular and as we headed up to Brenner Pass we were confident that we really would be able to enter Italy. But soon we came to an MP checkpoint where we received an unfriendly welcome. The MP's showed no interest in our enthusiastic desire to see Italy. It was made clear that they were there to stop everybody, civilians and military, from, entering Italy. They were specifically interested in the possibility that Germans, especially the hated SS men, disguised as American soldiers, might try to escape into Italy. This placed us in the category of very suspicious characters. Fortunately our leader had an authentic American accent in spite of his ethnic background and persuaded them that we were all red-blooded American G. I.'s Nevertheless we were not to be allowed to proceed. Turning back was a deep disappointment for the sergeant and other Italian-Americans in our party. It may have been a disappointment also for the steely-eyed M. P.'s who had surrounded our truck with their weapons at the ready. They looked as though they really wanted to open fire.

We wandered a bit on the return trip in order to see more scenery and visit the famous German towns of Garmisch-partenkirchen and

Oberammergau. Liberti turned out to be an excellent tour guide for this part of the world and the rest of the outing was enjoyed by all.

Fussen in Bavaria was the farthest point reached by the battalion. There we finally received orders to turn back to the North West. We were assigned as part of the army of occupation to the little town of Mosbach, near Heidelburg. Our motor pool came to rest in a garage for city buses. The buses had been re-located elsewhere leaving us with a commodious work area. We were billeted in fine new houses. Though these were of the German cracker box shape they were painted in a sandy pastel color and were really quite handsome. Rumor had it that they had housed Nazi big wigs who were now interned. I had a large private room on a second floor and there was a well-furnished parlor downstairs for our nightly bull sessions. We settled in, thinking it was only for the usual short term. We were destined to stay almost all summer.

CHAPTER 33

MOSBACH DAYS

The little town of Mosbach, in the German state of Baden, not far from Heidelberg, would have been a paradise for monks. Nestled at the foot of steep hills, on one side of a verdant valley, it offered everything the young men of Headquarters Company could have wanted, except feminine companionship. Fraternization was verboten. And the local girls knew what a strain it was for us and they delighted in enhancing the tension at every opportunity. For example, was it traditional for German farm girls to wear skimpy bathing suits while raking hay on the hillsides? Were road shoulders usually used for sun bathing, or was it only done along those routes where GIs passed regularly? And that leggy blonde in the white shorts, alleged to be the burgermeisters daughter, how many times each day did she need to walk down the main thoroughfare were bored soldiers were loitering? No doubt it was stressful for the girls too, with their own young men in PW camps or gone forever and the town full of strong, healthy, often handsome Americans in neat uniforms who were forbidden even to respond to a smile. But, of course, we did respond to smiles. The army could control our speech and most details of our behavior but it couldn't control the expression on our faces.

I had become accustomed to spending my Sunday afternoons alone, or with one or two companions, sitting in a meadow on a steep hillside back of the houses where we were billeted, reading, talking, or sometimes lying back in the sweet-smelling grass and clover to take a nap. I would drift off to sleep to the droning of the gentle bees. There were no chiggers or other biting insects, no thorns, no snakes. It was Eden and there was no serpent, but there was no Eve.

Recently I had fallen into an assignment which had altered my lifestyle in a manner I would never have imagined. There had been an announcement on the company bulletin board that instructors were needed for the Armed Services Institute classes which were to be taught in the local high school. Such classes were for the benefit of GIs who wanted to improve themselves or earn credit toward a high school certificate. Out of the whole company, only Harry and I and were chosen as instructors. He, our scholarly welder from Temple University, was to teach German, and I, the usually idle electrician was assigned to teach physics.

We were excused from duty at the motor pool and expected to devote ourselves to an imitation of the academic lifestyle. Imagine, getting up when you wanted to in the morning, putting on a good OD uniform instead of stained fatigues, spending the morning preparing lesson plans for only one hour of teaching, then, after lunch, taking a leisurely walk across town to the high school where a genial technical sergeant who had been appointed principal of the school was the only authority figure to be seen. The students were GIs from our own and other units stationed in the area. Whether they were there for self improvement or simply to escape the usual army busy work was something no one questioned. It was of course one small facet of a plan to keep the men of the army of occupation busy at something useful. There was only one strictly military requirement: Instructors and students were required to carry their carbines or Ml rifles slung on their shoulders as they went to and from the school. This, we supposed, was to continue reminding the German citizens that the American army was in charge.

After a few days I detoured past the motor pool one afternoon, on my walk back to quarters, to see how the old gang was doing. When I entered the German bus garage I found Sergeant Reggie seated on an upholstered living room chair, watching a German prisoner who was changing the wheel bearings on a GMC truck. Reggie's fatigues were spotless and his hands, even his finger nails, were clean. His face seemed plumpish as though he had gained weight. "Boy, you don't know what you're missing!" he said. "Everybody in the motor pool has his own assistant now. And are these guys good! Why, old Fritz here changes wheel bearings so fast I keep telling him to slow down."

Indeed, the motor pool area was full of toiling, serious-looking Germans and clean, relaxed GIs, presumably overseeing their work. I was not the only one with a new lifestyle.

But paradise was not without its problems. Sergeant Stroud greeted me with, "You should have seen what that dammed Joe did this afternoon. Actually, you would have heard the blast over at the high school if we hadn't caught him in time."

It seems Joe had been promoted to welder when Harry left. He had no qualifications or experience for the job but this didn't matter as he had an assistant, an expert German welder, to do the actual work. And, believe it or not, he had been promoted to T4 (sergeant technician) on the basis of the new assignment. Probably the master sergeant had pushed for the assignment and the promotion in an effort to get rid of Harry, permanently, since he had never liked him. Now, this afternoon, Joe had decided to play with the welding torch himself—his German assistant was working on another job—and he had set about repairing one of the harness hooks on the side of a truck bed. This involved heating a spot on the steel bed white hot, and Joe, true to his nature and reputation, had not bothered to look inside the truck to see what was on the other side of the metal he was heating. Fortunately the driver of the truck had come wandering on the scene—probably back from Heinie's Place—the secret, illegal beer joint that had sprung up in a nearby house—and when he saw what Joe was doing he started yelling, "Stop! stop!"

To quote Earl, "That idiot Joe was heating up the warheads of anti-tank rockets which were stacked with their noses almost against the side of the truck bed. Whether or not these rockets would have exploded from the effect of heat alone, Joe's failure to not observe their presence was the kind of error that would have broken him down to buck private if it had become known to our company officers. And it was possible that a few more minutes of heating could have caused a devastating fire or explosion. After this was brought to his attention all he could think of to say was, "Don't tell Sarge, you guys,you won't tell him will you?" His terror of the master sergeant was pathetic.

A few days later I visited the motor pool again on my walk back to quarters. It was late in the day, quitting time, and as soon as I walked in the master sergeant hailed me in a friendly manner which boded no good. He said, "Hey, Ed, I got a job for a man with a gun and you're the only armed soldier in the place." (I was called Ed, a lot. Simply an abbreviation for my last name stenciled on my helmet liner.)

I said, "Sorry Sarge, this ammunition clip is empty".

He said, "That don't make no difference. I gotta send uh armed guard with the truck that takes the Krauts back to their camp. They're good boys. They won't give you no trouble. Jist git in that three-quarter-ton and take a ride out to the camp and back."

The German prisoners assembled, climbed into the bed of the truck and arranged themselves properly on the seats along the sides of the bed. They were relaxed, friendly-looking men, mostly older then the average soldier, some in their forties I thought. Change their uniforms and haircuts and you couldn't have told them from GI's.

I was looking forward to a pleasant drive through the countryside. Then the driver appeared; it was Joe. He climbed in, chattering about nothing, as usual. He flourished his upper arm under my nose, almost rubbing his new T4 stripes against my face. I said, "It must be hell for you Joe that there's not a private left in headquarters company for you to boss around." He giggled and started telling me how great it was that the German prisoners were doing all the work. He didn't mention his own foray into welding a few days earlier.

We went roaring down the main street of Mosbach, Joe leaving the Dodge in a lower gear, perhaps because we were not supposed to exceed thirty five miles per hour, maybe just for the feeling of power the roaring engine gave him. Main Street led into a narrow, blacktop highway down a green valley framed by low mountains. Joe shifted into high gear and immediately exceeded the speed limit.

A difference between American and German soldiers now became evident. The whole gang in back burst into song. Their voices were really quite good. They sang a stirring marching song as the beautiful German countryside flowed by. As an additional bonus for me, Joe stopped talking. They sang two or three songs then lapsed into silence.

On a sudden impulse I hummed the opening bar of Lily Marlene. They took it up, almost reluctantly at first. Did they think I was mocking them? Did they know the song had become almost as popular among the allied forces as it was with the Germans? Now they lifted their voices and the song blossomed into its full splendor. There was a marching rhythm and at the same time sadness and longing. As I sat there listening— with goose bumps—it seemed to me they were expressing the longing and sadness of millions of doomed young men marching to their deaths in the snows of Russia or the sands of Africa.

Joe drove past the turnoff to the camp. The Germans shouted helpfully, pointing to the route he should have taken. He turned around in his seat exclaiming, "what? What?," and ran off the road into the shallow ditch.

I stepped down to the ground thinking, now, if ever, they will make a break for it! Foolish thought. A good American dinner awaited them in the camp, perhaps even a movie with Fred Astaire and Ginger Rogers. They cheerfully set their husky shoulders against the side of the truck and heaved while Joe spun the wheels. The truck came up onto the road again and we stood and watched while he turned it around. I was surprised that he didn't get at least one wheel into the ditch again.

The prisoners climbed aboard in the same orderly manner they had demonstrated earlier. We drove up the camp road to the gate where a bored MP directed us to the proper place to deliver our charges. The prisoners disembarked with military precision, dashed to a grassy area where an M. P. officer was waiting to call roll. They formed a perfect row facing the officer and came to attention with a clicking of heels. I would have liked to stay and listen to them respond to the roll call but Joe was eager to be off. The ride back to town was uneventful although I was probably apprehensive about Joe's newly reinforced reputation for bad driving.

CHAPTER 34

THE STRIPES MAKE THE MAN

I had noticed that Joe's new stripes had been crudely sewed on to his sleeves as if he had stayed up late under a poor light and sewed them on himself, his level of skill with thread and needle being somewhat comparable to his skill with the welder's torch. Haste in acquiring a new and higher symbol of authority is usually motivated by pride in the promotion but there is a practical reason for such haste and this was demonstrated after one of our moves to a new camp in the United states. On that occasion everyone had been issued new fatigues. These were the shapeless, green, cotton work uniforms that soldiers in those days never wore in public places outside of camp. Indeed it was widely believed that if a man did appear off base in such a uniform he would be mistaken for an escaped prisoner of war and apprehended by the local police. We may note in passing, that today, in the twenty first century, even generals with multiple gold stars pinned to their collars, appear in formal places wearing fatigues in various colors and patterns designed to furnish camouflage for deserts, jungles or halls of congress.

Now, on the day I am describing, we were introduced to our new quarters in a barracks building quite near to the mess hall. We were issued new uniforms and set about cleaning ourselves up and donning the crisp new clothes. After that we sat on our beds and talked, waiting for dinner. The highest ranking non-coms, staff sergeants and others usually decorated with multiple stripes, had chosen beds near the door. Apparently none of them saw any urgency about sewing their stripes on the new uniforms. Suddenly a fierce looking cook with a bristling mustache came through the door and stood glaring at the nearest men. As mentioned elsewhere, army cooks tended to be very macho in attitude and behavior. It was commonly believed that this was in compensation for their being engaged in what many soldiers considered women's work. Now the cook barked fiercely at a half dozen of the closest soldiers, pointing his finger at each in turn, and snarling, "You're on K P! Report to the kitchen right now!"

I am not sure how many stripes the cook was wearing. Most experienced cools were sergeants—wearing the same unadorned stripes worn by members of the training cadre, the three stripes that represented the right to command troops. But I am certain he did not out-rank any of the people he had now selected for K. P. duty. So what did they do, these high ranking men who had never expected to toil in an army kitchen again? They sat for only a few seconds exchanging surprised looks with one another, then, in a fine show of good sportsmanship, they rose up and walked humbly away to the kitchen. It seemed noteworthy that when they finally returned from work at a late hour some of them, in spite of their undoubted weariness, immediately set to work sewing stripes on their new uniforms.

CHAPTER 35

THE HAPPY EX-SLAVES

In mid summer something amazing happened, an announcement posted on the company bulletin board invited all of us to a dance to be held in the high school gym. It was sponsored by the British-run camp for displaced persons. We knew the inmates of the camp were former Polish slaves. Rumors flew that there were scores of blonde Polish girls who wanted to meet GIs. Since hope springs eternal in the breasts and other parts of lonely soldiers, we read the bulletin and went away dreaming of shapely Slavic beauties with friendly smiles and long blonde hair, all eager to thank us for rescuing them from their Nazi masters.

If there was disappointment on the night of the dance, you could not have told it by the expressions on the faces of the happy giants wearing U S uniforms, all leaping wildly to keep up with their tiny Polish partners in spinning, whirling polkas. Instead of potential Miss Polands, ready for an international beauty contest, we had plump, sunburned peasant girls with calloused hands, some of whom might have exceeded five feet in height if they had been miraculously provided with high heels. It was soon evident that Joe was in his element. Not only was he dancing the vigorous polkas expertly, he was talking excitedly to the girl in his arms. As he came whirling past me I heard him shouting over the music apparently entertaining the girl with one of his fascinating monologues. I couldn't tell what language he was speaking. My first partner, a tiny creature with an angelic smile, her red face lined beside the eyes from countless hours of squinting in bright sunlight, dragged me through my first lesson in how to dance the polka. It was hard to believe that these cheerful, smiling women had been slave laborers only a few weeks before. I wondered if slavery on a German farm had involved harder work or longer hours than the struggle to extract a living from a few bleak acres in Poland. And they looked as though they had been well fed. There was current story that some Polish men had run away from the displaced person's camp to go back to the farms of their German masters. This must have been a shock to the British personnel in charge of the camp.

After a couple of hours exhaustion began to take its toll and I decided to sand on the sidelines for a while and watch the scene. It was still fascinating with the foreign costumes and the wild dancing. Certainly the polish girls did not seem to be tired. And they would remember this night for as long as they lived. I could imagine them telling their grandchildren about the incredible night when the long years of drudgery on a foreign farm was followed with a night of dancing with American soldiers.

Joe had left the dance floor, at least for a while. I heard next day that he had been suddenly sick. Probably from too much Polish food—perhaps from sampling home made Polish liquor. In any case I noticed that the girl that he had been dancing with was now standing on the sidelines. I had noticed earlier that she was taller then the other women and did not have a sunburned face. I went over to where she was standing to ask her for a dance. I was thinking this might infuriate Joe when he reappeared and I was pleased with that idea. Now seeing her at close range, face to face, I was astonished at her exotic appearance. She was no outdoor worker—her face was very white, like that of a Finn or Norwegian. She had prominent Slavic malar bones that seemed to stretch her cheeks into flat planes on either side of her shapely mouth. Her straw-colored hair was abundant and fine textured, threatening to fly out of control. But most amazing of all, her icy blue eyes were slanted like those of a Mongol.

I tried to open a conversation using my faulty basic German which I thought she might understand—all of the slaves had to learn some German. I said, "Wo ist ihr Haus?" (Where is your home.) To my surprise she looked at me with a startled expression, as if I had said something improper---even frightening. Finally she said, in English, with what I thought was a rather charming accent, "When I am small—how you say—child—I am in Novosibirsk."

"But that's in Siberia," I exclaimed, "Are you Russian?"

She said, "I not want to answer questions ---I am in camp with Polskys—now I am Polski."

I said, "I'm sorry. I didn't mean to be nosy." I was baffled. Perhaps she had not expected me to know where Novosibirsk was. But why would she call herself a polski? That was a term of contempt the Germans had used for the poles they had reduced to slavery.

I said, "I know you did not work on a farm."

She said, "No, I not work on farm." I am doctor. In my country doctors are womans. In the war, I take care of soldier. When Germans catch me I go to *stalag* with other womans. I am doctor for other womans."

I learned her name was Amelia Anderson, a surprise at first but I reflected that it indicated a Scandinavian ancestor, perhaps one of those warrior Vikings who came down the rivers from the north and formed a ruling class in eight century Kiev. But those eyes told me another ancestor had come from far to the east. We didn't talk long for suddenly Joe was there, yelling in my ear, "Hey, are you trying to steal my woman?"

And to my surprise and disgust this intelligent Slavic Beauty was smiling with something like adoration at Screwup Joe. She actually held out her arms to him and he clasped her to his scrawny bosom and swept her onto the dance floor for another frenzied polka. It was a horrible sight, I thought, rather like the Hunchback of Notre Dame clasping the beautiful Esmeralda in his arms—something which she, a discriminating gipsy girl, never allowed while she was alive.

CHAPTER 36

PUNISHMENT

As mentioned earlier, I had become accustomed to spending my Sunday afternoons alone, or with one or two companions, sitting in the meadow on a steep hillside above the house where we were billeted. Now on this day, shortly after the dance with the Polish women, I was up there, sitting on a bench, when Sergeant Stroud came along and sat down beside me. I had been reading but he wanted to talk, so I closed my book. Conservation with a friend would pass the time as well as reading.

After a while, three Polish girls from the displaced persons camp came strolling along the path. Their hair was done in Gravel Gerty style, their clothing suitable for scarecrows, but they had friendly smiles. I recognized them from the dance at the high school the previous Friday. Stroud, every ready for a laugh, called out the ridiculous sounding greeting which we had heard Joe use. Picking up strange girls was not something one would have expected of Stroud--he was one of those ever-faithful family men, devoted to wife and children, who had never been known to seek feminine companionship since our earliest days together in the Arkansas training camp. But now he called out a hearty "yok-she-madge" and the girls responded with giggles and a flood of unintelligible Polish. Seeing· our expressions of incomprehension they switched to the Lingua Franca of the late Nazi realm— simple basic German. They were a merry group, much given to giggling and when Stroud asked them if they knew Joe they chorused "Ja Ja" and one of them began to tell

155

her companions something in a rapid and excited manner. Their wide eyed reception of this information, and their Polish equivalents of ohs and ahs, led us to believe that shocking gossip involving Joe was being recited. One of the girls translated in basic German for our benefit. I caugh the phrase, "Joe war am das bett mit Marie." Stroud said, "Did she say what I think she said?"

Soon the girls wandered off and we devoted ourselves to planning how we could utilize the information we had just received about Joe's amorous activities with the unknown Marie to bring him maximum embarrassment. Actually, I doubted that he would be embarrassed rather than accept the scandal as evidence of his manhood. And how did the Russian doctor, whose name I had learned was Amelia, fit into this story? When last seen she had certainly seemed to be accepting Joe as an exemplary specimen of American manhood.

Our speculation and planning was brought to an abrupt halt by the appearance of someone running up the trail that led to our bench, a military figure with multiple stripes flashing on his sleeves as he swung his arms like a sprinter in a track meet. As we sat there wondering what could inspire such vigorous activity on a warm afternoon we recognized the top sergeant of Headquarters Company. His three stripes up and three stripes down on each sleeve accounted for the conspicuous flashing we had noticed from afar. Now he came charging along the path to our bench and came to an abrupt halt. He puffed and panted for several seconds before gasping out, "You guys are in real trouble!"

He then revealed that he had been ordered, by a phone call from the battalion commander, to identify two soldiers who were fraternizing with German girls on our hillside. He said, "The Colonel is over there in a house across the valley, looking through powerful binoculars. He can see everything that happens over here."

Of course we both protested with righteous indignation that the girls were Polish, from the displaced person's camp, the same girls we had been allowed to dance with the previous Friday. And didn't the Colonel himself sign that announcement of the dance which appeared on our bulletin board?

The Top Kick was obviously moved by the vehemence of our argument. He said, "Well, I'll do what I can for you guys. I think the

Captain knows you two are about the least likely to get into trouble of anybody in the company."

If that was a compliment we both failed to thank him. In fact we were left wondering just how we had acquired the status of Goody Two Shoes. I remembered that Stroud's nickname was "Bucky", a name reserved for those who are seemingly trying to impress the brass in order to get a promotion. Actually he was simply a remarkably talented master of many skills—a design machinist in civilian life. He always tackled any assigned job cheerfully, often doing more than he was expected to do. As for me, there had never been any evidence that the captain, the company commander, knew that I was alive. Maybe he was impressed that I was teaching physics. Maybe he had enjoyed my letters that he had censored the previous winter.

Apparently the top sergeant relayed our arguments to the Captain who then presented our case to the Colonel well enough to avoid severe repercussions. But the rumor came down to us that the battalion commander had asked, how did they know the girls were Polish, not German? Apparently his binoculars were not of top quality. No German girls would have gone out of their homes dressed and coifed like those three.

So we were both assigned to extra duty. This was only a night of guard duty, from which we non-com technicians were usually exempt. We suspected it was a symbolic punishment to save face for the Colonel. After all, no commanding officer should ever admit to enlisted men that he has made a mistake.

Harry sized up the situation in his usual pedantic manner. "The Colonel," he said, " is a very lonely man. He has no peers for companionship, only officers of lesser importance. What can he do to pass the boring hours on Sunday afternoon? Well, he can scan the hillsides with his binoculars, and who knows what entertaining activities may be underway on yon grassy slope? At least, you and Earl remained seated on the bench, or so you say, not rolling in the grass with the three witches of Warsaw.

I pointed out that this last was an unkind statement. Those innocent Polish girls had been deprived of all training in cosmetology, hair styling and the selection of appropriate clothing. Their German masters had wanted them to look like slaves; they had had no choice in the matter.

I reported for guard duty. It was the usual training camp arrangement of four hours on, four hours off—continued for twenty-four hours. Theoretically one was supposed to sleep during the hours off duty, but since I was to start walking my post at twenty hundred hours, this would be a night of little sleep and much weary walking. But much to my surprise I was assigned to the entrance of a ten pitched in the middle of a vacant lot where one lonely prisoner had to be guarded.

I had heard that we had a company prisoner but I had not known who he was or the nature of his offense. The man in the canvas-walled guard house was a friendly, talkative New Englander with a surprising collection of books and a philosophic attitude toward the fate that had brought him to this disgraceful situation. He invited me to come into the tent and sit down, a courtesy I declined, at least until darkness fell. For all I knew, the colonel with his faulty binoculars was somewhere this side of the horizon, checking me for military perfection. I had no desire to be gigged for dereliction of duty by failing to walk up and down in front of the tent in a military manner, as prescribed by one of those guard rules which every army recruit has to memorize. I did this for a while, marching stiffly with the carbine at right shoulder arms and doing snappy about faces at the end of each straightaway, but soon darkness shrouded the area and I sat down on the threshold of the tent, which had a raised wooden floor, and engaged in a companionable conversation with the prisoner.

He was really quite a nice fellow. His downfall had come upon him with stunning swiftness. A month earlier he had been "shipped in" as a replacement. This meant he had been sent, alone, to join our outfit. The fate of an individual replacement was always a dreaded one. A soldier can face really frightful conditions so long as he has the support and fellowship of familiar companions. But a single individual, sent alone to join strangers, is often under severe psychological stress. Not only is he being placed in a situation where he knows no one and knows nothing of the usual routines, he is also likely to be assigned at once to the most undesirable tasks the new unit has to offer. This man had arrived at our company headquarters late on a Saturday afternoon. After dinner, assuming he had no duties to perform, he had set about lowering the level of the schnapps in a bottle he had been carrying in his luggage. After sinking into a soothing doze on his newly assigned bed, he was startled to hear the top sergeant bellowing his name, and to find that he was being assigned to guard duty in the unfamiliar German night. We were ensconced at the time in pleasant houses on an attractive street in the German resort town of Goppingen. The war had been over for only a few days and the possibility of a last stand by Nazi forces in a Bavarian mountain redoubt had not yet faded away. So sentries were assigned to pace up and down the streets outside the buildings in which soldiers were sleeping. Electric power had not yet been restored so those streets were very dark.

Why the sergeant did not perceive that the new man was in no condition to be walking guard with a loaded rifle in such surroundings was a point conveniently overlooked at the subsequent court martial trial. To make a long story short, our prisoner had lost his nerve while patrolling a pitch-dark street and had fired a shot at a threatening enemy who was purely a figment of his intoxicated imagination. For firing his rifle on a peaceful German street he was sentenced to several months' confinement at hard labor.

Since the battalion had no guard house, Headquarter Company was required to retain custody of the convicted man. This involved extra duty for the men who had to guard him, for company administrators who had to plan his daily "hard labor," and even for the cook who had to provide for his meals apart from the other men. The prisoner seemed not to have a care in the world—he had plenty of leisure time for reading his books and writing letters home, and an endless succession of guards with whom to converse. It seemed to me he might well be the most relaxed man in Headquarters Company.

CHAPTER 37

HOMEWARD BOUND

The quiet summer in Mosbach ended early for us. At the end of July an order came for our battalion to depart for an unknown destination. The rumor began to circulate that we were being sent to the Pacific theatre to participate in the invasion of Japan. Our battalion commander assembled all of us in the high school auditorium for an emotional farewell. Sorrowfully he announced that our Engineer Battalion was being disbanded. The men in the front rows reported tears on his cheeks as he made this somber announcement. It was scarcely a surprise, as we had been designated as security police shortly after V-E day and had spent some time cruising about in sleek armored cars, prepared to play a new role of keeping insubordinate citizens in line. . The vehicles were supposed to inspire awe in any civilians who had decided to rebel against army rule. Of course, there was no such rebellion—not even a hint of one—so the armored cars soon disappeared—probably shipped to the Pacific to awe the Japanese after that war was over.

The good news at this time was that we were to be sent home for a lengthy furlough before being shipped to the Pacific Theatre. Again I heard that oft-repeated saying of soldiers in war: "If I can just go home for a couple of weeks I don't care what happens after that."

I was scheduled to leave with the first contingent. On the cool morning of the second day of August I carried my duffle bag, heavy with extra clothing, a camera and a few precious books, over to company headquarters. Baggage and men were being loaded into trucks ready for departure. Some of the men who were scheduled to leave later gathered around to see us off. It was the last time I was to see many of my friends. We promised to write to one another when we got home. We from the western states took dignified leave of one another with casual voice and stoic expressions. The men of the first service command (New York and New Jersey) were noisy as usual, slapping one another's backs, shouting affectionate farewells like "Write to me you bastard!"

Soon we were driven away. Striking the main road to Heidelberg our trucks turned north along the beautiful, winding Neckar River, past forests with their trees planted in neat rows. Women were working in the fields, older women in long black dresses, their heads protected from the sun by black scarves, young women, perhaps demonstrating the Hitler Youth obsession with being tanned and fit, favored shorts and halters. Or perhaps they dressed that way to titillate the passing soldiers, some of whom always yelled or whistled their appreciation for this kind of roadside entertainment. Apparently this was not considered fraternization, as we heard of no orders prohibiting such behavior.

We drove through Heidelberg, which was relatively undamaged, much later through Mannheim where we saw again the results of mass bombing. We drove past great mounds of broken bricks and masonry, the remains of collapsed buildings. Women and children were scrambling over these artificial hills, apparently searching for something useful or valuable. Three months had passed since the bombing ceased but we saw no evidence that rebuilding had begun. After a while we rode the autobahn, later a temporary road—probably constructed by our engineers—paralleling damaged strips of the autobahn. Once we bypassed a fallen bridge, great slabs of concrete dipping into the water of a river. But many small towns through which we passed seemed undamaged.

We arrived finally at a replacement depot near Marburg where we were housed in six-man tents, each of us with one of those folding cots of wood and canvas that had been used as extra beds and camp beds ever since the first world war. The rains started almost at once. We spent days lying on those cots listening to the rain rattling on the tent over our heads. We would get up for a dash to the mess tent three times a day, then lie down and go to sleep again. I never knew an adult person could sleep so much. I am not sure how many days this lasted.

During one break in the rain I went for a walk among the tents and paused to look into one where gambling had been in progress, it was said, for days. Men were clustered around one of the cots where money was displayed and dice were being thrown. The tent was so full of smoke it was pouring out the door as if from a chimney.

My notes show we arrived in the Marburg camp on the night of August second and departed by train on the thirteenth. On night there was a show featuring among other acts a scantily clad girl tumbler. There was a peculiar crowd reaction to her performance. I had seen the same act months earlier, probably in Mosbach , and during that performance the men in the audience had whistled and yelled their appreciation of the nearly-nude girl's contortions. Now in this performance, for men who would be home in a few days, there was almost no reaction, most of the audience just sat and watched in silence.

But the thing that looms largest in my memory of Marburg is that shortly after August 6th, the news spread that a new kind of bomb had been dropped on a Japanese city—a bomb so powerful that the whole city had been destroyed. One of my tent mates declared he had been at Ft. Belvoir when that new explosive was tested. He claimed to have witnessed several test explosions, exclaiming, "Boy, that stuff is really powerful." I knew enough about any possible "atomic bomb" to know that it had not been tested in a camp inhabited by thousands of men. Perhaps the man had actually witnessed some kind of explosives being tested, or was he one of those peculiar people who claim they are already aware of anything new they are told. Years later I had a teacher colleague of whom it was said, if you told him a complete fabrication such as, "A meteor hit the city hall in Los Angeles last night" he would respond, "Yeah, I heard about that!"

There were a few rainless days at Marburg. On one of these we sat in a field and were briefed by an officer about our coming furlough in the States. We were to be free for thirty days---an incredible vacation from army life to be anticipated with real joy. And we would be sent to one of two engineer camps, Ft. Belvoir, Virginia, or Ft. Leonard Wood, Missouri, to which we would return after the furlough. This confirmed that we were still engineers in spite of the dissolution of our former battalion.

From Marburg we went by train to Camp Top Hat, near the port of Antwerp. This was a torturous ride as we were in French railway cars fitted with hard wooden benches. These cars bore faint, faded inscriptions: "forty men, eight horses." This was a famous caption remembered by veterans of World War One. It seems that old freight cars never die, at least not in France. Along the way we observed, with considerable resentment, British troops reclining in comfortable seats in large American style railway coaches. I suggested these luxurious travel accommodations may have been brought over from Canada, which uses railway equipment similar to ours. We also passed one train packed with Russian soldiers, presumably former prisoners of the Germans, now being returned to their fatherland. Their railway cars were decorated with festive greenery, leafy branches and flowers, but our friendly waves were not returned. They simply stared at us blankly. Had their propagandists been briefing them on the evils of American capitalism? Or did they have some inkling of the fate that awaited them in Stalin's Domain? We later heard that all Russian solders who had surrendered to the enemy were considered deserters and faced summary execution upon arrival in their homeland.

Near the Belgian border our train rolled across a landscape that had been cratered by countless explosions. The land was almost bare of vegetation and I thought it odd that, in the whole summer that had passed since the allied armies had fought their way through this area, few weeds had grown in the tortured soil. Had the explosives poisoned the soil so that nothing could grow there or had even the weed seeds been killed by the shock, or heat of explosions?

Farther on, we crossed a wide river on a newly constructed railway bridge. British engineers were working on the approach to the bridge and one of our humorists yelled out the window, "Oh, my god, the Brits built this bridge! We're all going to die!" The British engineers stared at us almost as coldly as the Russians had.

We arrived at Camp Top Hat near the port of Antwerp on the fifteenth of August. All I remember about Antwerp at that time was that the Dutch, with their obsessive neatness, had built walls of the bricks from fallen buildings so that the ruins would be concealed from people walking along the streets.

Three days later, we boarded a liberty ship for the journey back to the United States. Everyone's morale was high. Crowded conditions on board the ship could have been depressing but we were headed home—nothing could bother us now! This turned out to be not quite true. Emerging from the English Channel into the open Atlantic, we encountered stormy weather with strong winds and high waves. The ship pitched and rolled and virtually everyone on board became sea sick. I thought it strange that this happy crowd could be so stricken. Perhaps the bad food conditions contributed to the problem. We who were still able to eat had to spend a good part of the time standing in line in order to receive the two meals a day we were allotted. I cannot recall sitting down at a table to eat at any time during the homeward voyage. As a reward for waiting in line for what seemed like hours we were handed a snack to carry away. The bad weather soon cleared up, but this only made the food problem worse. Now there were many more people able to stand in line. After ten days of this near-famine we arrived at Boston on the 28th of August.

I remember the arrival in Boston harbor as if it were yesterday. Some ships blew their whistles in welcome and a large boat, probably a ferry, came out to meet us with a dance band blaring jazz and a crowd of girls on its deck, gyrating wildly to the music. Soldiers on our ship yelled their approval. As we walked down the gangplank onto the dock, a greeting committee of older women handed each of us a quart of milk. I drank all of mine and soon began to feel sick. After ten days of starvation my shrunken stomach was in no condition for a whole quart of symbolic mother's milk. Actually I was unable to consume a meal of normal size for at least a week during which time I arrived home in Kansas and alarmed my mother with my inability to consume all she set before me.

CHAPTER 38

A LETTER FOR BUBA

I saw Buba for the last time the day we arrived at Camp Miles Standish. His tiny dog had run into the street where cars were passing and he was yelling from the curb for the dog to come to him. He had somehow managed to smuggle that dog From Mosbach to Marburg, then to Camp Top Hat, and amazingly he had hidden and fed it on the crowded troopship across the Atlantic. I reflected that now, if it survived the auto traffic here in the Boston area, one more train ride would bring the French dog to a new home in the mountains of North Carolina, a place called Coon Holler. The affection of the big, rough man for his tiny dogs was, it seemed to me, his redeeming virtue.

Later that same day I was in a booth in the camp PX, drinking a coke and reflecting on the joy of being back in the United States, when suddenly Buba was there, looming over me. He was accompanied by a burly companion who somehow managed a rustic appearance even in uniform. Buba handed me a somewhat crumpled sheet of writing paper and said "Kin you tell me if this says whut I think it says?"

The letter was from France. The language was simple, the cursive script a challenge. As I deciphered it, I seemed to see again that dreary little town in Lorraine where we had been billeted for a while in early March. We had soon learned why the local citizens regarded us with a sort of sad aloofness. The first American troops to enter the town had been a cavalry regiment, scouting ahead of our main forces in fast armored cars. They had been met by joyful, flag-waving, French inhabitants and their glowering German neighbors. It proved to be a premature celebration of liberation. The Americans moved on and a few hours later a German unit, withdrawing toward the east, surged through the town, pausing just long enough to pound on the doors where French or American flags were flying. Whoever opened the door was instantly shot.

The letter had been mailed in that sad town. Its theme was of another kind of heartbreak. "Now that the war is over," she wrote, "I pray every day that you will come back to me. The baby is beautiful—he is big—will be a big man like you—I pray, always, that soon he will see his father. "

The burly companion slapped Buba on the back, and shouted jubilantly, "Yer a daddy! Hey, You have to give me a cigar!"

Buba, beaming proudly, said, "let's go get beers—Ah'll pay for yers." They turned to leave.

I called after them. " Don't you want the letter?" Buba hesitated, then came back, snatched the letter and thrust it, unfolded, into his pocket. They went off to their celebration, talking loudly, laughing boisterously, like athletes after a winning game.

EPILOGUE

I suppose a woman would have seen the flaw in that letter right away. Being a man it took me several days. In fact I was riding west on a transcontinental train, half way to Kansas, when boredom led me to extract the small, worn notebook from my pocket and review the record of our European travels. I saw that we had been in that sad little town, from which the letter was mailed, in mid February. The letter had been mailed in mid august. I suddenly caught myself counting on my fingers in the manner practiced by Joe. After that I sat up straight and exclaimed in a manner that led my seat mate to inquire "What's the matter?" Six months isn't long enough I said. She had said, " the baby is beautiful. He is big. He will be a big Man like you." Premature infants are not big. They are not even beautiful, not at six months. And they usually don't survive. That big beautiful infant had been sired by someone else while Buba was still separated from France by the English Channel. That girl wanted an American husband! But of course she didn't know about Coon Holler. Imagine a French woman taking that long journey as a war bride, expecting bright lights, a shiny car, a modern kitchen like the one she had seen in a movie. But she finds herself in Coon Hollor with kerosene lamps, a woood-burning cook stove and an old ford truck. Well, first of all it would never happen. Men of Buba's ilk did not travel back to Europe to collect a foreign bride. Second, it was no affair of mine. I shifted my body in the train seat and tried to go to sleep.

More loose ends need tying up. What happened in the matter of Marie, the one bedded by Joe, and Amelia, her successor? According to scuttlebutt and speculation Joe had promised both of them, successively, marriage and a free trip to America. He had tired of Marie, transferred his attention to the more attractive Amelia, and the angry Marie had reported to camp authorities that her successor was a Russian imposter, pretending to be a Polish citizen to escape repatriation to Stalin's tender mercies. I hope this is not true. I hope Marie merely said "Good riddance" and Amelia's value as a trained physician was recognized somewhere. But the world of war prisoners from Eastern Europe was a cruel place. There was little reason to hope for happy endings. Again, it was no affair of mine. The safety and security of peacetime America was wrapping around me. It was best to forget about people I could not help.

And besides, in one matter of great importance I could not even help myself. Phone calls to Lovely Frances in Virginia were usually answered by her mother who said, with evident relish, "Frances is not here. *She is out on a date.*" She knew we were engaged but she did not approve. I even suspected my letters were being intercepted. To make a long story short, Frances married her current, persistent suitor. He was a navy man, an officer, his uniform was better looking than mine. But more important, he was there, while I was being held in army limbo in far away Missouri.

I had planned to enter George Washington University in the fall to work on a higher degree. Instead I did what many Kansas boys do—I went west. To Colorado first, where the young lady from Newton eventually joined me, then to California where I spent most of my professional life. Many times during my teaching career I found an early dictum useful: Never volunteer for anything!